Harry Bertoia, Printmaker

Photograph of Harry Bertoia from the announcement of his 1977 exhibition at Fairweather Hardin Gallery, Chicago, Illinois. I am indebted to Sally Fairweather for this photograph.

Harry Bertoia, Printmaker *Monotypes and Other Monographics*

JUNE KOMPASS NELSON   Wayne State University Press   Detroit   1988

Great Lakes Books edition copyright © 1988 by Wayne State
University Press, Detroit, Michigan 48202.

92 91 90 89 88   5 4 3 2 1

Library of Congress Cataloging-in-Publication Data

Nelson, June Kompass.
    Harry Bertoia, printmaker.

    (Great Lakes books)
    Bibliography: p.
    Includes index.
        1. Bertoia, Harry—Catalogues raisonnés.
2. Monotype (Engraving), American—Catalogs.
3. Monotype (Engraving)—20th century—United States—
Catalogs.   I. Bertoia, Harry.   II. Title.   III. Series.
NE2246.B47A4   1988   769.92′4   87–32780
ISBN 0-8143-1964-5   (alk. paper)
ISBN 0-8143-2063-5   (pbk.: alk. paper)

This publication has been supported in part by a grant from the
Michigan Council for the Arts.

It necessitated inner vision to take over the function of
the eye.

Harry Bertoia, *Fifty Drawings*

PATRONS

George Bedrosian

Kaare Berntsen

John Booth

Fairweather Hardin Gallery

W. Hawkins Ferry

Sally Gilbert

P. C. Hartmann

Robert L. Kidd

Robert and Evelyn Snyder

Makepeace Tsao

T. K. Zung

Contents

Color plates begin on page 48

Foreword

In recent years a continuing phenomenon of exhibitions of prints by contemporary artists has been the preponderance of works in monotype. In reaction against the machine-like perfection of the workshop prints of the two previous decades, a new aesthetic sensibility has emerged in the 1980s which values the unique effects of the transfer process and favors the media of monotype over the editioned print. We refer, here, to the monotype in the plural because there are so many variations possible in this most flexible means of producing prints. In her careful analysis of Harry Bertoia's innovative printing methods, June Nelson has defined the special properties of the monotype and the appeal which this technique—with its inherent spontaneity—had for a visionary artist like Bertoia. In fact, in order to find a suitable term to define many of Bertoia's sheets, Nelson has added a new word to the vocabulary of printmaking—*monographic*.

The publication of this study of Bertoia's monotypes, or monographics, coincides with a contemporary preoccupation with the medium and enlarges upon an ever-deepening interest of art historians and collectors in American art of the middle decades of this century. The Detroit Institute of Arts celebrated this period in the exhibition *Design in America, The Cranbrook Vision 1925–1950* (December 14, 1983–February 19, 1984). Harry Bertoia was first a student and then a teacher of metalwork and printmaking at Cranbrook from 1937 to 1943. He began working in monotype in 1940—nearly a decade before his first attempts in three-dimensional sculpture—and continued to make prints throughout his career until his death in 1978. He created over a thousand monotypes, the majority of which remained in his studio and are kept together today by his widow, Brigitta Valentiner Bertoia. Of these, seventy-nine, which are representative of his principal styles and themes, have been selected for discussion in this publication and for exhibition. Relegated to the background as Bertoia became known for his furniture designs and for his sculpture, the monotypes have not been exhibited as a group in themselves since 1947.

Both Bertoia's graphic works and sculpture were briefly discussed in the catalog for the Detroit Institute of Arts' Cranbrook exhibition. His sculpture had previously been examined in depth by Nelson in her book *Harry Bertoia, Sculptor* (Wayne State University Press, 1970). Thus, while Bertoia's stature and accomplishments as a sculptor have been established, until the publication of this second study by June Nelson, the astonishing extent, variety, and richness of his work in the graphic media had not been revealed.

The Department of Graphic Arts of the Detroit Institute of Arts is pleased to have this opportunity to present this unique exhibition and to have a scholarly publication to accompany it. We extend our thanks to June Nelson for her dedication to this project, to Brigitta Valentiner Bertoia for her cooperation in lending the works for exhibition, and to the staff of Wayne State University Press for making this book available for our exhibition.

Ellen Sharp
Curator of Graphic Arts
Detroit Institute of Arts

Acknowledgments

This book had its beginnings, in my mind at least, in 1966, when Harry Bertoia first showed me some of his graphics and told me of the techniques that produced them. At that time I remarked that they would make a great book. In 1969, after my first book, *Harry Bertoia, Sculptor,* had been accepted for publication, I specifically asked Harry for permission to write about the prints. He said, "Not yet." I saw him from time to time during the seventies and mentioned it once or twice, but the answer was always the same.

Then, suddenly, he was gone. At least, it was sudden to me as I had not seen the Bertoias for more than a year prior to November 1978. The following year I wrote to Brigitta Bertoia proposing an undertaking such as this book and was refused again. It was not until late 1980 that she wrote to me suggesting it might be possible now if I were still interested. I was.

The research was considerable, in terms of both the prints themselves and the details of Harry's life. First, there was the selection of a limited number of the graphics from among those left to Brigitta. Then came the arduous process of dating them. Brigitta Bertoia was particularly helpful here. Nemo Warr, with the help of a grant from the Michigan Council for the Arts, did a fine job on the photography. Finally, it was necessary to study the prints minutely in order to be able to write about them. This study required recourse to an art printshop, made available to me through the kindness of Wayne State University's Department of Art and Art History, where I tried out a few of Harry's techniques to see how they worked. I also consulted printmakers—notably Tom Woodward and Bob Broner of Wayne State University, and Steve Murakishi of Cranbrook Academy of Art—whose advice was freely given. John Gerard, former Director of the Cranbrook Academy of Art Museum, was both helpful and encouraging, as were Bernard Goldman and Richard Kinney of Wayne State University Press.

As I sought more and more information with regard to Harry's thoughts and philosophy of life and the influences thereon, I was grateful to have completely at my disposal the files remaining from his studio, which Brigitta and Val Bertoia very generously allowed me to keep at my home for several years. Conversations ensued—frequently with Brigitta and other members of the immediate family; with Harry's three nieces, Alida Bertoia, Marie Griffith, and Deli Vetere; with Clifford West, Elfriede Fischinger, Lydia Winston Malbin, Ray Eames, Sally Fairweather (who produced an extremely helpful set of tape-recorded conversations she had had with Harry shortly before his death), and many others who were generous with their time.

I am grateful to the readers of the manuscript—including Brigitta, Val, and Lesta Bertoia—all of whom made worthwhile suggestions, as well as to the editor, Michael K. Lane, who honed my prose without injuring my feelings.

Most of all, I am grateful to my husband for his patience and understanding through many years of frustrations and deadlines. His unfailing encouragement and the undeniable beauty of the graphic works themselves have spurred me to complete this book in tribute to Harry Bertoia.

1. Introduction

Recognized throughout the United States and in many parts of Europe for his furniture designs and welded-metal sculpture, Harry Bertoia also produced an important body of work in the printmaking field which is less well known, but even more remarkable.[1] It consists of monotypes and other unique forms of the graphic artist's craft made throughout his career, from 1940 until his death in 1978.

Taken in historical context, the Bertoia graphics of the 1940s represent one of the earliest sustained interests in the monotype and related printing techniques in this country in modern times. Their origin preceded by more than a decade the general revival of interest in printmaking in the United States, which occurred in the late fifties and sixties. It preceded by twenty-eight years the intensification of interest in the monotype in the United States evidenced by the proliferation of exhibitions of works in that medium after 1968. As prints go, they tend also to be larger in actual dimensions than most monotypes produced before the 1960s, although in the early years there is considerable variation in the size of Bertoia's works, and some are quite small indeed.

Many of the planographic printing techniques developed by Bertoia are unique to the point of defying positive identification, having been developed in his studio by experimental methods. Although he had no contact with others in the field, the few printmakers who have seen his works are impressed by his results in color and tonal values and are often frankly puzzled as to how they were achieved. It is hoped that study of them in these pages may reveal their secrets and inspire the creation of new techniques by monotypists of the end of our century. The importance of many of the prints as unique works of art has been recognized over the years through acquisition by museums in various parts of the country.

Each Bertoia print is unlike any of the others, since none was reproduced in an edition. They are never reproductions of other, larger works in another medium. Rather, each is a spontaneous, individual work of art, born afresh each time out of the whole cloth of the artist's imagination, brought to life in a matter of minutes or hours, not days. Historically speaking, the entire group of graphics done from 1940 to 1978, numbering well over a thousand, may represent the largest body of unique prints ever produced by a single artist—an artist, be it mentioned, whose major source of income was derived from another medium, sculpture.

Bertoia learned the technique of monotype by trial and error, as do most artists who take up the medium. Not only was he self-instructed in printing techniques generally, but throughout his forty-year career he never made the acquaintance of—let alone worked with—any other printmaker. Although graphics workshops were set up in a few cities under the auspices of the Works Progress Administration of the Federal Government, professional printmakers and art-printing shops of the Parisian ilk were nonexistent in the United States until the coming of Stanley William Hayter's Atelier 17 to New York City in 1940. This studio, which attracted the war-displaced European surrealists and a few U.S. artists (such as Alexander Calder and Jackson Pollock briefly, and Mauricio Lasansky more influentially), was devoted to intaglio printing, a very different technique from that adopted by Bertoia. No doubt he was aware of Hayter's work through articles such as one in a 1941 issue of *Art News* that reproduced some of the Englishman's paintings and prints.[2] There is no question that they both used some aspects of surrealist automatism to help form their images, but Bertoia's printing methods as well as his intent (and, consequently, his results) were unlike Hayter's. Hayter used automatism to set the overall linear pattern for each of his prints, then elaborated on it in a variety of controlled ways. Bertoia often let his hand wander from the beginning to the end of his process, which rendered it impossible to see the result clearly until the pulling of the one and only print from the plate. Hayter returned to Europe in 1950, but his workshop continued for a while and "the vitality of his technical approach swung the focus of American printmaking to intaglio, where it remained throughout the forties and fifties."[3] Bertoia, on the other hand, continued experimenting with his own individualized method of planographic printing.

In speaking of printmaking in the first three decades of this century, one writer says, "The status of the American print was not generally acknowledged. Collectors and the larger museums often preferred the prints of established European artists."[4] Another writer has said that "the graphic work that painters, sculptors, and professional printmakers produced throughout the forties and fifties went largely ignored by all but a tiny segment of the public."[5] The great wave of interest in printmaking did not come into fruition in the United States until the 1960s. By this time the legacy of Stanley Hayter, through Lasansky and others, had brought forth traditional gravure print shops in many parts of the country. The establishment at the beginning of that decade of the Tamarind Lithography Workshop in Los Angeles completed the renaissance. Several times in the history of the latter organization, June Wayne, its founder and director, wrote Bertoia urging him to set aside time for a Tamarind fellowship.[6] He declined, making the excuse that he planned to spend the summer in Europe—which he did not do (and perhaps had no intention of doing).

Neither Tamarind nor Atelier 17 would have been right for Bertoia, whose prints were produced by neither intaglio nor lithographic process. He always worked alone rather than with professional printmakers, by choice hand-printing his graphics, without benefit of press, and devising new methods and implements as the need arose. As Hayter himself remarked in his book, *About Prints*, there is a "tendency for free workshops to disappear and for any serious invention, if it is found at

all, to arise from the work of individuals isolated in their studios. . . . It must be obvious that . . . the expressive possibilities of a process in the hands of an artist who has himself devised it can give results in the category of the print as a major work far beyond any result to be expected from the ingenious adapters of other men's methods."[7]

Of further historical importance, the images in Bertoia's first graphic works of 1940–43 represent not only an awareness but a wholehearted acceptance of avant-garde European art movements, which was unusual for his time and place. They reveal a commitment to ideas of both geometric nonobjectivity and lyrical automatism that did not become the norm in the United States until after the Second World War. Even Lionel Feininger, a U.S. artist who was resident in Europe from 1890 to 1937, showed an influence only from cubism in his works. And Una Johnson says of Feininger's prints, "He is the only American artist whose work gives recognition to the major art movements in the first half of the twentieth century."[8] In the twenties and thirties, only a very few U.S. artists espoused the modern movements, and those who did tended to gravitate to centers like New York City rather than remain isolated in the U.S. heartland. Without his having actively or even consciously declared allegiance to such theories, Bertoia from the beginning produced images that demonstrate an early link between constructivism and surrealism in the United States.

Constructivism was largely a sculptor's style and had been practiced from about 1913 by European masters such as Vladimir Tatlin, Alexander Rodchenko, Naum Gabo, Antoine Pevsner, and László Moholy-Nagy—the latter a Bauhaus affiliate, founder in 1937 of the Institute of Design in Chicago, now part of Illinois Institute of Technology. Its Russian adherents were closely allied with the painter Vladimir Malevich, whose theories of suprematism led to his own and Wassily Kandinsky's geometric works. An offshoot of cubism's concern with the interpenetrability of space and matter, constructivism strove for purity of line and simplicity of structure. It promulgated strict nonobjectivity, and its attributes consisted of a tautness of both angular and curving lines and simple geometric forms held in precise and careful balance. A major objective was to make space visible by emphasizing it in airy constructions of plastic, metal, and wood.

Surrealism, too, beginning in 1924, strove to make visible the invisible by the artist's automatic setting down on paper or canvas his subconscious images or dreams without the intervention of conscious thought. Also a European style, its major practitioners were André Masson, Max Ernst, Joan Miró, René Magritte, Yves Tanguy, and, later, Salvador Dali and Paul Delvaux. For the most part, these painters' works were based on reality. The meandering lines and irregular shapes of some of their more abstract evocations, however, such as those by Masson and Miró, are almost the antithesis of the constructivist aesthetic. Bertoia may have learned of these movements from reproductions in art magazines in the late 1930s. He must have been as fascinated with the precision and scientific bent of the one as he was with the visionary aspects of the other. His earliest nonobjective images are either precisely geometric or loosely linear or a combination of both, floating on spaces of indeterminate depth. Their debt to these earlier twentieth-century art styles is immediately apparent, although his works are by no means slavishly imitative. What is of particular interest and importance is his amalgamation of the two rather divergent theories, along with another concept of his own concerning the continuity of change, while working in more or less of a vacuum in the U.S. midwest.

A poor, non-English-speaking Italian immigrant at fifteen, Bertoia knew soon after he graduated from Cass Technical High School in Detroit in 1936 that he could no longer depend on the teaching of others to determine the direction his art would take. Instructors at both the School of the Society of Arts and Crafts (which he attended on scholarship for one year) and Cranbrook Academy of Art in Bloomfield Hills, Michigan were unsympathetic to the new mode. The Gallery of the Society of Arts and Crafts, while it attempted to bring modern art into the cultural life of the city, defined such art as beginning with the impressionists and never mounted an exhibition of nonobjective twentieth-century art. When the works of Paul Klee were shown in 1940, the exhibition was not well received.[9] The Detroit Institute of Arts, under the directorship of William R. Valentiner, was already collecting Matisse and the German expressionist painters, and these works were exhibited from time to time. But there was only limited exposure to avant-garde European movements in the 1930s in the industrial metropolis of Detroit. In spite of this, Bertoia embraced with eagerness such twentieth-century ideas in art as nonobjectivity, automatism, and space-time relationships, and worked untiringly and experimentally toward these ends from 1940 on. At arts and crafts-oriented Cranbrook he was almost alone among instructors in his enthusiasm for these advanced theories. In fact, he received nothing but discouragement for his initial printmaking efforts from Eliel Saarinen, the chief administrator at the school, who, when Bertoia timidly showed him some prints, advised him to stick to his metalwork. (A few years earlier Saarinen had referred to the modern German paintings shown in the catalog of Hitler's show of "degenerate art" in Munich in 1937 as "revolting canvases.")[10] Only a few colleagues recognized the worth of Bertoia's prints until their acceptance by the Solomon R. Guggenheim Foundation's Museum of Non-objective Painting in 1943. His sale of over one hundred works to that museum was accomplished through the mail, without his ever having set foot in New York.

The Museum of Non-objective Painting opened in New York City at the end of May 1939. Its first exhibition, which included works by Kandinsky, Moholy-Nagy, Léger, Gleizes, Picasso, Nicholson, and Gris, among others, was well received by the reviewers for New York-based art magazines.[11] Throughout the 1940s the museum was well patronized by the New York art community, as had been the occasional truly contemporary exhibitions at the Museum of Modern Art, which opened a decade earlier. Artists in other parts of the country, however—especially those with Depression-drained resources—were limited, in their exposure to these works, to the occasional black-and-white reproduction accompanying the magazine reviews. Exhibitions circulated by the Museum of Non-objective Painting to "small museums, schools, and even civic organizations" seem not to have reached Cranbrook.[12] Instead, in 1940 the Academy cooperated with *Life Magazine* in the mounting of a large exhibition, "Contemporary American Painting." Fifty artists were represented, all of them more or less devoted to realism.[13] Significantly, the more avant-garde U.S. artists, like Arthur Dove, Stuart Davis, John Marin, and Georgia O'Keefe, were not among those selected. The first exhibition to come to Detroit including works by the likes of Kandinsky and Mondrian, was arranged by a ceramics student at Cranbrook, Lydia Winston (later Malbin) for the Women's City Club of Detroit, of which she was a member, in May 1942.[14] By this time Bertoia had already committed himself to the notion of nonobjectivity. However, it may have been through Mrs. Winston, an avid collector of futurism and other styles of modern art, that he first learned of the existence of the Museum of Non-objective Painting and its director, Hilla Rebay. The latter was the first person of authority to give him real encouragement to proceed along the lines of his early experiments. Nonobjectivity was in the wind in the United States at this time, to judge from the "hundreds of artists and would-be artists" who sent their work to Rebay for criticism and advice in the years immediately following the opening of the museum.[15] But it had not been so for long. There had been, in the twenties and thirties, a "close commitment to reality that characterized not only most American painting in general but American cubism [the most prevalent style of the early modernists] in particular."[16] Those U.S. artists who had been inclined toward nonobjectivity in the second decade of the century, such as Arthur Dove, were persuaded away from it in the twenties, in part for patriotic reasons, and in the thirties for more practical reasons. This began to change in the early forties, and Bertoia was in the forefront of his colleagues in his wholehearted acceptance of the trend away from reality.

The historical achievements of Bertoia take on even greater implications when it is realized that they were accomplished by one individual working alone rather than as part of a collective "school" of art sustained by group contacts. The late thirties and early forties were, in the words of Thomas Messer, director of the Solomon R. Guggenheim Museum, "a pregnant moment in American art history," leading, as they did, to the development of the first internationally recognized school of art to originate in America—abstract expressionism.[17] But only a few artists yet embraced with complete enthusiasm the concept of nonobjectivity, and those who did resided for the most part in the East in close proximity to one another, so that their ideas were constantly subjected to cross-fertilization by their associates. Bertoia, on the other hand, worked out his own techniques and compositions without recourse to informed criticism or group discussion. At Cranbrook no one else seemed interested in printmaking and of the two painting instructors, Zoltan Sepeshy remained tied to realism all his life and Wallace Mitchell lagged behind Bertoia in adopting the nonrepresentational. Bertoia's friends at Cranbrook for the most part were not other painters or printmakers but the architects from whom he learned to respect Bauhaus principles of design.

In the early forties, New York-based artists were just beginning to react to the influx of surrealist artists exiled from the war in Europe, whose only U.S. group exhibition was held in New York in the fall of 1942. It was several years before abstract expressionism (generally considered to be a result of contact between the European surrealists and the younger U.S. artists interested in abstraction) was born in that city in the work of Arshile

Gorky, Jackson Pollock, Robert Motherwell, Willem de Kooning, Mark Rothko, and others. In a reflection of what was undoubtedly the spirit of the times, Bertoia's development preceded and paralleled theirs. There are major differences, however, between the work of Bertoia and that of the abstract expressionists. In the beginning, at least, he insisted on nonobjectivity, while they rejected a complete separation from reality.[18] His imagery is not one of violent self-expression such as characterized much of their work. Rather it has a gentle, poetic quality that differs considerably from the slashing strokes and angry coloration of his New York contemporaries. Perhaps most important, Bertoia's two-dimensional work is in the print medium and not in painting, a conscious choice that limited both size and coloration to dimensions more suitable to its sense of intimate visionary revelation.

Abstract expressionism, the United States' first original "school" of art, a style that became often, although not exclusively, nonobjective, dominated the 1950s—a decade *after* Bertoia's adoption of such imagery. But "few Abstract Expressionist painters were concerned with making prints in any medium."[19] Jackson Pollock made a few prints at Atelier 17 in 1944, but they were never exhibited until 1967, long after his death and well after the establishment and acceptance of the abstract-expressionist style. These have been described as having "achieved through the method of automatism some of the first dynamic and expressive compositions that were to characterize the early mode of American Abstract Expressionism."[20] Bertoia's interest in printmaking had begun at Cranbrook in 1938 or 1939 as an outgrowth of painting and drawing, which he studied while working as instructor in metalcraft. His results of the early forties, clearly showing, especially in his more linear works, his adaptation of the accidental image derived from automatism, were exhibited in New York in the summer of 1943 at the Museum of Non-objective Painting. Jackson Pollock worked briefly there at that time as a "custodian and preparator of paintings."[21] Pollock could not have failed to see Bertoia's works that summer and, given his own bent toward the nonobjective, it is not unlikely that they had some influence, if only in sending him to see Hayter for a try at what the printing medium could produce for him.

As a group, the Bertoia graphics reveal an artistic personality that was quiet, humble, thoughtful, sensitive to concerns of the twentieth century, yet free from blatancy or opportunism. They evidence none of the flamboyant attempts at self-expression seen in the painting of the New York School. They are not concerned with popular styles and their rapid shifts—from abstract expressionism to pop to op to postpainterly abstraction—which occurred during his lifetime. Rather they are concerned with an inner vision of the world around us, past, present, and future—a vision presented with humor and optimism. They are poetic, mysterious, evocative. They expand our perception of the universe. They amuse in a gentle, yet provocative, way. They intrigue us with shadowy nuances and suggestions of dreamlike origins. Whether the images are precise and geometric, or softly curving and spontaneous, they present a lyrical expression of rhythmic form and line analogous to the harmonious qualities of music. And since the sounds of a new, otherworldly kind of music were often very much in the artist's thoughts, the analogy is an apt one.

Bertoia's graphics were consistently one of his major preoccupations. It was through his prints, in fact, that his talent was brought to the attention of the art world. They received enthusiastic reviews in New York early in the 1940s, a decade before his first serious attempts at sculpture were exhibited. And they continued to hold the position of "first love" with the artist, even though much of his time in later years was consumed in the conception and production of sculpture. In fact, there was contant interaction between his graphics and his sculpture. Not only did he sometimes make the prints in order to work out elements of three-dimensional design, but he referred to them often as source material. The contrast between his precise metalworking techniques on the one hand—whether for small-scale jewelry or large-scale commissions—and the freedom with which he worked the prints on the other brought a freshness to both mediums whenever he switched from one to the other. For Bertoia, his "drawings," as he sometimes called them, were a form of relaxation, as well as a statement of aesthetic principles requiring frequent renewal or refreshment. Throughout his life, rarely did a week go by without recourse to the printing plate.

Apart from their historical value, the unique prints resulting from the nearly four decades of Harry Bertoia's working life have an intrinsic value that is apparent in both their imagery and their technique. The essence of their images is that of a truth beyond the truth of nature. In this they are of epic proportion—epic in the sense of being out of the ordinary, larger than life, more meaningful than would at first seem to be the case. The extraordinary originality of motif is unique to Bertoia, unidentifiable with either previous or contemporary art or nature. The biomorphism adopted by so many of the surrealists is not present in Bertoia's works. Neither is the unrestrained splash and splatter of some of the abstract expressionists. Where geometry is present, a feeling of static dryness is not only avoided but is turned into a sensation of flickering movement through rhythm and line. His interest in space-time relationships led to many works done in series showing the growth of an idea from inception to fruition, a kind of "mobile painting," as he called it in a letter to Hilla Rebay.[22] These series prints are particularly interesting because of the way they permit us to enter the brain of the artist to watch it work as his imagination develops variations on a theme.

In what may seem a paradox in view of their apparent freedom of execution, Bertoia's graphics are also notable for their craftsmanship. Each repetitive, freehand line, each sinuous stroke, each delineated form, each fortuitous blob conveys a sense of the confidence with which it was incorporated into the composition. It is this sureness of stroke in combination with the originality of idea and spontaneity of execution to which these graphics owe much of their charm. Technique and imagery become one in the totality of the individual work of art. Their originality of image and a technique incorporating both textural variety and a wide range of tonality rank these works among the finest prints produced in the United States in our century, albeit they remain essentially unknown to modern U.S. monotypists. Undated by representational details, Bertoia's graphics have a timelessness about them that is reflected in the themes they imply. Untitled, they nonetheless suggest hauntingly large concepts—cosmic space, primordial time, infinity, eternity—which reach out from the artist's inner vision to stimulate our own.

Why, then, in view of their quality, their originality, and their timelessness, have these works been largely ignored except by a few museums and collectors? There are several reasons.

The first might be referred to as "the monotype fallacy." Until 1968, when Degas's monotypes were exhibited in an eye-opening show at the Fogg Art Museum, dealers, collectors, and museums were often reluctant to handle monotypes because they are unique prints, not part of an edition. For dealers, the lack of an edition to sell meant an obvious loss of income. Collectors, except the courageous few, wanted corroboration of their judgment in the form of fellow collectors owning the same work. Museums were reluctant because there were not many monotypes (artists, too, usually preferred the edition for monetary reasons), and they were impossible to classify with works in other print mediums. Consequently, "Many national print shows . . . caution artists that 'all print mediums are accepted except monotype.'"[23]

A corollary to the monotype fallacy has been the problem of nomenclature, which will be taken up at greater length below. Suffice it to say here that museum personnel, dealers, and artists themselves were often confused as to what to designate works of such an experimental nature as most modern monotypes. Those of Bertoia, when they were first exhibited in New York by the Museum of Non-objective Painting, were miscalled "monoprints." Sometimes they have been referred to as "paintings," other times as "drawings."

A second reason has to do with the general unpopularity of "total abstraction" in the United States during the first half of the twentieth century. The derision that greeted the 1913 International Show of Modern Art, seen in New York, Chicago, and Boston, has been well documented. In spite of its poor reception, however, it focused attention on cubism, and this style proceeded to inform the work of a few modern-minded U.S. artists during the teens, twenties, and thirties, John Marin and Stuart Davis most notably. Arthur Dove was all but alone among U.S. artists in the early years in following up on the European notion of the totally nonrepresentational in art, and his paintings of this ilk were not often shown to the public. Economic conditions brought on by the Great Depression forced a return to realism by most artists, who could not afford to ignore the wishes of what few patrons there were. It was not until the forties that knowledge and conditions combined to bring forth considerable interest in nonobjectivity, and even then it was a slow learning process, generally speaking, for both artists and public.

With the emergence of the New York School of abstract expressionism in 1945, there arose an emphasis on painting in which vivid colors and vigorous brushwork covered increasingly large canvases that overshadowed the more subdued art of the printmaker. In 1947 Bertoia's graphics ceased being shown in New York, possibly in part for this reason and certainly for another reason: his gallery went out of business that year as a result of the death of its owner. Soon after, his work, first as a designer of chairs and then as a sculptor, became well known, and his prints, a much more personal art form,

were relegated to the background, only occasionally gracing the walls at exhibitions of his sculpture or furniture.

From 1952, the showrooms of Knoll International, the design and furniture manufacturing firm with which he had become associated, exhibited Bertoia sculptures and occasionally his graphics also. His name thus became associated with modern design and its commercial outlets, showrooms, places not frequented by artists, critics, and museum curators with the same regularity as museum and gallery exhibitions. The association with Knoll continued throughout his life on an informal basis long after he ceased designing for them. While it was a friendly arrangement for both, it may have been a drawback to the serious consideration of Bertoia's art by those who found it thus commercially tainted.

The first one-man show of Bertoia's sculpture mounted by the Fairweather Hardin Gallery in Chicago in 1956 included a number of graphics. A Smithsonian traveling exhibition of 1956–57 entitled "Recent Work by Harry Bertoia" included twenty-five graphics, although its focus was on chairs and sculpture. The American Federation of Arts' "Forged in Fire" of 1957–58 showing the new metal sculpture of Bertoia, Herbert Ferber, David Hare, Ibram Lassaw, Seymour Lipton, and Theodore Roszak included three of Bertoia's monotypes, along with drawings by each of the other artists.

Although several museums throughout the country own Bertoia prints, they have not been exhibited by a museum in a group for themselves alone since 1947. Because of his lifelong reluctance to sell them, the individual prints tended to accumulate and were preserved in a system of cabinetry set up in Bertoia's home studio. It is from this personal collection that the seventy-nine works reproduced here have been culled.[24] The selection is meant to represent the graphics area of Bertoia's creative endeavor in all its variety both of conception and technique and throughout all phases of his career. An attempt will be made to categorize the prints according to their chronological place in Bertoia's oeuvre and to analyze them in terms of their technical and aesthetic components.

Definition of Terms

In the discussion of Bertoia's graphic works that follows, some of the words used will require explanation. While monotypes are becoming increasingly popular among artists in the latter part of our century, the general public remains somewhat unfamiliar with the term.

The word *monotype* appears to have been coined about 1880 for an artist's printmaking process (and the resultant print) invented in the seventeenth century.[25] Giovanni Benedetto Castiglione, a Genoese contemporary of Rembrandt, actually invented two methods—one in which a picture was painted directly on a plate and a second in which the plate was covered with ink and the picture was scratched or wiped out of the inky background —each of which, alone or in combination, when transferred by pressure to paper, was capable of producing a single print.[26]

Actually, it is usually possible to produce at least a second and sometimes a third, much paler impression. Michael Mazur, one of the contemporary artists working in the medium, puts it this way: "However the monotype is made, it is characteristic that some residue is left on the printing surface after the print is taken. Second prints of this lighter image are called 'cognates' for their kinship with the first impression. . . . these cognates play a special role because they create a new set of tonal values to which new material can be added."[27] It is this feature of the monotype process which gives rise sometimes to works done in series, each succeeding print being unique in its additions to the ghostly remains of the one before, not a repetitive duplicate as in the editions produced by other printmaking processes.

About the same time Rembrandt was having his first success as a painter in Amsterdam, Castiglione was in Rome experimenting with rapidly inking and printing his unetched plates to achieve maximum tonal and dramatic effects. The process did not catch on widely in the seventeenth century, however, which was perhaps even more interested in maximum distribution than in tonality. It was not until the late nineteenth century when impressionist and postimpressionist artists sought textural variety, visible brushwork, and rapid development of an idea that the process, now dubbed monotype, became popular. It fell into disuse again in the early 1900s to be revived popularly only in the latter part of our own century.

The word derives from the Greek *mono* (single) and *type* (impression), a reference to the fact that the process reputedly allows for only one good impression and that each print is therefore unique. Not everyone has been pleased with the term, however. Degas never used the word, preferring to call his works in this medium, many of which were finished with additions in pastel to the surface, "printed drawings made with greasy ink," a rather cumbersome appellation.[28] Bertoia was never completely satisfied as to what to call his works, referring to them variously as "drawings," "monoprints," or, in later years, simply "graphics."

In modern parlance, *monotype* is often confused with the word *monoprint*, which did not reach the dictionaries until *Webster's Third International*. There it is given a definition that only adds to the confusion by being almost identical to that for *monotype*.[29] Artists and art historians, on the other hand, have long used *monoprint* to mean an ink impression produced by any of the traditional processes, to which some additions or changes have been made, varying it somewhat without basically differentiating it from all the other prints in its edition.[30]

The confusion surrounding the word *monotype* as far as twentieth-century artists are concerned stems from the basic simplicity of the technique, the experimental nature of most artists who take it up, and the attempts on the part of curators and others to narrow the definition. Henry Rasmusen, the first author in the United States to discuss the monotype at book length, states that after considerable study he "is tempted . . . to say that *a monotype can be almost anything.*"[31] He then proceeds to qualify from the general definition, "a monotype is a planographic print form leaving no residual plate," until he reaches this detailed definition:

A monotype is a unique, printed impression produced by painting a picture or design on a plain surface, such as glass or metal, and transferring it to another surface, such as paper or cardboard.

According to this, there are four points of distinction between a monotype and other kinds of prints: (a) the completion of painting first, (b) on a plain (unincised) surface, (c) the transference to another surface, and (d) its singularity. The more exactly any finished print comes to fulfilling these requirements, the nearer it approaches to being a true monotype.[32]

This attempt to purify the monotype definition is an attempt to distinguish the process from that of all other kinds of prints—etchings, engravings, woodcuts, serigraphs, and lithographs—for purposes of classification. The difficulty lies in the reluctance of artists to be classified. Especially in the twentieth century, their experiments with tools and materials diversify the results often beyond recognition of source, let alone classification.

Most writers on monotype are careful to admit the role of experimentation. Rasmusen says, "At this time in the history of the subject the combinations of methods and materials becomes [sic] so varied that the term 'monotype' can no longer be applied to much of the finished work, unless anything done by an indirect, freehand, transfer method could loosely be said to come under this heading."[33] Colta Ives, in "The Modern Art of Monotype," says of the artists who practice it, "The urge to experiment, the need to explore every possible way of visually expressing themselves is pervasive in this company and is the single greatest factor in their adoption of the monotype technique."[34] Experiments have led to such variations of the process that artists searching for a word accurately to describe the technique used and/or its result have come up with such suggestions as *multitype, monogouache, monopainting, monopen, texture imprint, prototype,* and *floatagraph,* to name a few.

What most clearly characterizes what we call mono*types* today is what distinguishes them from mono*prints:* there was never any intention on the part of the artist to print the image in quantity. A mono*print* can be an etching, an engraving, a woodcut, a serigraph, or a lithograph —any printed work that can exist in an edition—so long as it has been treated in some way individually by the artist. But a mono*type* is incapable of being reproduced in an edition. It can be reproduced only once or twice after the first proof, and the second and third printings are mere ghosts of the original to which, more frequently than not, new material is added to produce a totally new image.

I have therefore chosen to adopt a new term, *monographic,* to designate a unique print, made by a planographic process, of a freehand drawing or painting, the original of which is so depleted in the transfer process as to be incapable of further complete reproduction. This definition is meant to be inclusive rather than exclusive. It includes all works produced by transfer printing so long as they are unique, that is, impossible of reproduction in an edition. It includes the "true monotype" satisfying Rasmusen's four conditions, as well as all other planographic-process prints of an individual nature. It distinguishes these works from all other traditional graphics and allows for the inclusion of the many experimental methods being used today and others yet to be invented. Further, it makes clear that this particular form of graphic is the only printed work to be produced solely for the sake of the artistic result—the particular effects that can be achieved only through the transfer process—and not even obliquely for the pecuniary purpose of duplication. A monographic is truly an individual work of art, as is a painting or a drawing, not one of an edition of ten or of one hundred or of five hundred.

In the end, the value of any work of art lies not in its

technique, though this is often of interest, but in the quality of imagination the artist projects through the image. As William M. Ivins, Jr. puts it, "The only two techniques that really are of artistic importance . . . are those of pictorial imagination and sharp-sighted, sensitive draughtsmanship. No one can ever be taught these two great techniques, for they are part of the eternal mystery of personality and its growth, to be recognized but not to be rationalized or reduced to a method. They can no more be imitated than wit."[35] The imaginative, sharp-sighted, sensitive, and sometimes witty monographics reproduced here give full evidence of their artistic importance and that of Harry Bertoia as one of the most original artists of the twentieth century in the United States.

Dating the Monographics

Although they were highly regarded and carefully preserved, none of the monographics was signed or dated. Bertoia deliberately did not sign any of his work—sculpture or graphic—because he felt that to do so was indicative of possessiveness. The idea of dating them apparently never occurred to him. They were produced rapidly, and he was constantly moving on to new ideas evolving out of the old. Furthermore, he continued to use the graphics, from time to time pulling them out to look over ideas of the past in the light of new work he was continually producing. Occasionally he would even reprise an old theme, many years after its original conception, changing it and developing it further. When the old works were returned to storage there is no assurance that they were put back in their original place. Then, too, his generous nature caused him occasionally to be prevailed upon to sell or give away an admired work. And since his death, of course, there has been a dispersion of some of the monographics among his heirs in the settlement of the estate.

For all these reasons, the problem of determining precise dates for the prints is an extremely difficult one. It is impossible, except in a very few instances, to do more than group the prints by decade. In some cases even that has to be conjectural, as the work of one decade may resemble that of another.[36]

Criteria used in the dating process were various. First of all, the present location of some of the works owned by others was taken into account. For instance, the Cranbrook Academy of Art Museum now holds fifty-one Bertoia prints, all of which are known to have been done by 1943. Of these, forty-one were acquired direct from Harry Bertoia prior to his departure for California that year. The remainder came to the museum in 1979 from a private donor, but these, too, are known to have been executed before Bertoia left Michigan.

The eighteen prints now at the Solomon R. Guggenheim Museum are the residue of the well over a hundred Bertoia graphics they once owned. These consisted of an original group purchased by curator Hilla Rebay in April 1943, one acquired March 26, 1945 (probably from the Nierendorf Gallery in New York), and thirty-one acquired from the purchase of the Nierendorf estate and accessioned January 1, 1948. All of these were retained for thirty years or more by the Guggenheim.[37] From time to time some of them were loaned for such purposes as a traveling exhibition in 1951–52 and exhibitions at various museums, colleges, and universities during the fifties.[38]

In 1978 negotiations were initiated by the Guggenheim Museum to exchange a number of the monographics for a sculpture. Delighted at the prospect of having the prints back, Bertoia arranged for three sculptures to be sent them from which they could choose. The agreement was finally consummated in February 1979, three months after his death, when 109 graphics were returned to the Bertoia estate. Some of the latter may be among the works exhibited in this publication.

The single monographic owned by the Museum of Modern Art is a composition of geometric forms, and as such it is characteristic of many of those produced in the early 1940s.[39] It was probably purchased from Nierendorf. There are also Bertoia monographics dating from the forties at the Wadsworth Atheneum, Hartford; Munson-Williams-Proctor Institute, Utica, New York; Addison Gallery of American Art, Andover, Massachusetts; and the Los Angeles County Museum. Private collectors now living in various parts of the country also own early works (one in California was known as late as 1964 to possess fourteen or fifteen). Some or all of these may eventually find their way to museums.

Comparison of these externally datable graphics with the works at hand has helped to date the latter. Some of the works of the fifties, sixties, and seventies can be dated by association with specific sculptures whose dates of completion are documented. Association with specific events in Bertoia's life—the births of his children, the deaths of close friends and family members—has dated others. Still other criteria include an analysis of the earliest known use of certain motifs, as well as of specific drawing implements. Bertoia experimented with several kinds of the latter, whose marks can be identified on the prints, and certain implements are known to be associated with particular periods in his life. Lastly, but often most effectively, the types and sizes of paper used become clues to dating, especially where it can be deduced that certain sizes and types were most frequently used at particular times. A pattern of paper usage thus helps date many of the works. Despite these various criteria, the dating of some of the graphics even by decade remains insecure. There is, nevertheless, a certain cohesiveness about the decade-by-decade grouping, and a great deal can be learned from a chronological examination and analysis.

2. Biography

The Early Years (1915–36)

Born in 1915 in a small town near Udine in northern Italy, Harry (Arieto) Bertoia experienced a more or less normal European rural boyhood. His earliest remembrances associated with cultural experiences were those of listening to music played by the elders in his family. He always preferred drawing to playing with other children, although he was well liked. "I always knew the world of art was the one I wanted to be part of," he said.[1] What instigated his first art instruction was his copying at the age of eleven or twelve of a hundred-franc note so precisely that it could not be distinguished from the original. It so impressed relatives in the United States, where it had been carried by a friend of Harry's father, that pressure was exerted at home to give him further training, and he was enrolled in evening drawing classes.[2] A few years later, he and his father entered the United States through Canada to join his brother Oreste, a factory worker in Detroit.

Bertoia arrived in Detroit in 1930 in the depths of the Depression. Soon his father returned to Italy, and Harry and his brother lived on the twenty dollars a week Oreste could earn at that time. Nevertheless, Oreste insisted that instead of looking for a job, Harry become educated, and he was fortunate enough to gain admittance to Cass Technical High School with its special program for talented students in the arts. The trip to school took him one-and-a-half hours, each way, by public transportation, but it was well worth it. It was there that he made contact with two exceptional teachers, Louise Greene and Mary Davis, to whom he later gave considerable credit for having "a marvelous understanding of all of the arts," presenting their material "in a beautiful way," and being "very open-minded."[3] At Cass Tech he learned a lot of drawing, some painting, and jewelry making with various materials—silver, copper, ebony, some stones. A painting from the 1930s of a lantern-lit night scene with figures and horse-drawn carriages, possibly a remembrance of Italy, shows considerable mastery.[4]

It was Greene who insisted that he should get a scholarship on graduation, first to the Art School of the Detroit Society of Arts and Crafts and later to the Cranbrook Academy of Art in Bloomfield Hills, Michigan. It was Greene, also, who drove him, with his portfolio and a little box of jewelry, to the interview with Eliel Saarinen, president of that institution. He was hired on the spot to reopen the metalworking shop that had been idle since the departure of Arthur Neville Kirk during the economic crisis of 1933. So it was that Bertoia went to Cranbrook on a scholarship in 1937 to study painting and teach metalcraft, and he remained there until 1943.

The Cranbrook Years (1937–43)

Little came of his formal scholarship study. As he told it years later, he attended only a few classes in painting with Zoltan Sepeshy, and none in sculpture, although he often talked with Carl Milles there. "As I grew, as I entered Cranbrook," he observed, "I began to feel that guidance was not sufficient and that I had to rely much more on my own investigation. . . . I tended to break away from disciplines such as a class of drawing or a class of weaving. I began to jump the fence to see what was on the other side. I began to look at other facilities. . . . Investigating the possibilities of the print shop opened up a new path."[5]

By 1939 Bertoia had taught himself printmaking techniques by dint of working six hours at night after his daytime duties teaching metalcraft were discharged.[6] As a result, when metals became increasingly difficult to obtain because of the war, he was assigned to teach graphics for the 1942–43 school year.

The studio workshops were perhaps the most vital contribution to art education made by the Cranbrook Academy of Art, which was at that time, in the words of Eliel Saarinen, its architect and first president, "not an art school in the ordinary meaning. *It is a working place for creative art.* . . . Creative art cannot be taught by others. Each one has to be his own teacher. But (contact) with other artists and discussions with them provide sources for inspiration."[7] The emphasis on contact, discussion, and creativity was the elder Saarinen's brainchild, based on his experience with Finnish and German art movements, and it governed the educational experience provided by the Cranbrook Academy of Art in those days. "Right away," Bertoia said, "we began to hear of the Bauhaus and other schools and what was happening in such centers. . . . One begins to benefit from every direction."[8] The particular period when he was in residence at Cranbrook included the time when "the school had entered a golden age. In fact, the two academic seasons before the American entry into the Second World War crystallized the magic of the place. The foundation laid by the older masters inspired and supported the new energies and ideas of the younger faculty and students."[9] Recalled Bertoia, "It was among the very best times of my life."[10]

The domination of the Cranbrook Academy of Art by Eliel Saarinen assured its emphasis on architecture, however. This was particularly apparent in the visiting artists who were invited to lecture or confer with faculty and students. There was not one painter or printmaker among them during the years of Bertoia's residency. Most prominent among the luminaries who did put in an appearance on campus were Frank Lloyd Wright and Walter Gropius.

Bertoia's most stimulating contacts in those years at Cranbrook were with his colleagues—Benjamin Baldwin, Ralph Rapson, Florence Schust (later Knoll), and Harry Weese, architecture students; Maija Grotell, ceramist; Carl Milles, sculptor; Charles Eames, at first a student and later in charge of the department of design—as well as the entire Saarinen family—father and son Eliel and Eero, architects; mother Loja, weaver; and daughter Pipsan

Saarinen Swanson, designer. Most of them became and remained his good friends. While at Cranbrook they influenced and were influenced by each other in one way or another, and their lives continued to be entwined in later years even though in some cases they seldom saw each other after leaving the school.[11]

It was in 1940 that Bertoia met and later courted Brigitta Valentiner, a student at Cranbrook and the daughter of William R. Valentiner, then director of the Detroit Institute of Arts. Contact with Dr. Valentiner's fine private collection of drawings and paintings by twentieth-century European artists was an eye-opening reinforcement of Bertoia's early imagery.

Success came soon to Harry Bertoia.[12] His unusual designs were popular, and he sold a fair amount of silver jewelry to his Cranbrook colleagues from time to time. His early success culminated in 1943, a very important year in his life. In this year he first sold some of his monographics to Solomon R. Guggenheim's Museum of Non-objective Painting, which exhibited them in New York City that summer; had a successful show and sale of jewelry and prints at Cranbrook; got married in May; and left Cranbrook for the West Coast in October.

The sale of over a hundred monographics (then called monoprints) to the Guggenheim was direct. Bertoia simply packed them up and sent them where he thought they might be appreciated, and they were. The exhibition in New York that summer generated a great deal of interest, as well as several reviews particularly complimentary to Bertoia's contribution. For example, the following:

While the show included such well-knowns as Moholy-Nagy, Hilla Rebay, Werner Drewes, Charles Smith, and several others, it is clear that at least two of the artists who share the largest representation on the walls have been invited for the summer display with especial confidence. Harry Bertoia, a relative newcomer, who has nineteen woodblock [*sic*] designs in color, of which several are marked as recent acquisitions, uses musical terms to describe his subjects. He works with precise but graceful line and delicate color and usually avoids the somewhat general "geometric" classification into which the exhibited work falls. . . . The display . . . offers the largest presentation of contemporary non-objective art by Americans which has yet been given by the Museum.[13]

The show and sale at Cranbrook took place just before he left for California. It included both jewelry and monographics. Many of the geometrically oriented works were framed in copper with glass on both sides. They were meant to be hung in a window to take advantage of the transparency of the oriental paper on which they were printed to enhance the three-dimensional effect of the overlapping forms. The linear works were more simply matted for display. A number of prints were sold, as well as a considerable quantity of jewelry. The Cranbrook Academy of Art Museum acquired forty-one graphics at this time, some of them purchased and others as a gift from Bertoia. Graphics were also sold to private collectors in the area. The sale provided the young Bertoias with a nest egg for their move west.

As a result, at least in part, of the Museum of Non-objective Painting show in 1943, Bertoia established a connection with the Nierendorf Gallery in New York that lasted until Karl Nierendorf's death in 1947.[14] The gallery gave regular showings of his jewelry and monographics (again, usually referred to as "monoprints"), and from 1945 to 1947 Nierendorf subsidized Bertoia in the amount of two-hundred dollars per month in exchange for a regular supply of his work. When Karl Nierendorf died, the Bertoia prints still in his possession were acquired by the museum, the name of which was changed after the death of its patron in 1949 to the Solomon R. Guggenheim Museum.

In California (1943–50)

Harry Bertoia's California period came about as a result of the collaborative success of two of his Cranbrook colleagues. Eero Saarinen and Charles Eames working together won two first prizes for furniture designs in the "Organic Design in Home Furnishings Competition" held at the Museum of Modern Art in 1940–41. That same year (1941) Eames and his wife, Ray (a Cranbrook alumna), moved to California to continue experimenting with using molded plywood in chairs. Having considerable difficulty with the design in 1943, they persuaded Harry Bertoia, as well as other Cranbrook cohorts, to come and lend their assistance. This was a year of change for the Cranbrook Academy of Art as well. Wartime shortages of materials, particularly metals, were making it more and more difficult to maintain the workshops, while at the same time the departure of male students to join the war effort made for decreased enrollments. New, stringent requirements became necessary as the academy evolved into a degree-granting institution. These facts no doubt helped bring about Bertoia's decision to accept the challenge and move to the West Coast.[15]

During the first years in California, the Bertoias enjoyed living in the lower part of a small beach house, while Harry worked with Eames at the Evans Products Company on war contracts, as well as on molded plywood furniture designs. When it became apparent that some metalwork was required, Eames sent Bertoia to a school to learn welding. The work on the chair was finished in 1945. When the resultant design was exhibited at the Museum of Modern Art in 1946, it became known as "the Eames chair." Disillusionment ran high among those who had worked with Eames, each of whom had made a contribution and had been led to believe he would share in the credit.[16] One by one, they left.

The Bertoias moved first to Topanga Canyon and in 1947 to La Jolla where Harry gained his United States citizenship and worked as a draftsman at Point Loma Naval Electronics Laboratory until 1950. Two of their three children were born in California, and it became necessary for him to provide a steady income for his family, especially after his stipend from Nierendorf ceased. Throughout this period, however, he continued to produce his graphic works regularly as well as to initiate sculptural works of metal rods and wires.

When he arrived in California in 1943 Bertoia began immediately to perfect the rapid-drawing technique he had instituted while still at Cranbrook, using printer's ink and a glass plate. The linear works he had produced back east were the prototypes for further exploration into the possibilities of the medium. Working at home in the beach house night after night, he experimented with different implements and various methods of obtaining an inked print.[17] It was at this time that he began to realize the importance to him of these daily exercises, and he began to take a more cautious approach to parting with the results of his efforts.

Until 1947, of course, he continued to send some completed work regularly to Karl Nierendorf in New York. Early in 1945 one reviewer wrote that Bertoia

confirms himself as one of the most inventive and original of the non-objective painters. . . . tremendously varied textures as well as design itself, animate his work. . . . Line varies from spidery to one which has body—swirls around, sometimes used like a cage enclosing space. The forms have the look of pieces of glass, turning in different planes. Opacity and transparency, two- and three-dimensionality, and subtly variegated color are used with such skill that each print has its own life and sets its own mood.[18]

Later that same year, his monographics were exhibited at the San Francisco Museum of Art (now the San Francisco Museum of Modern Art), and from 1944 until he returned east, they were occasionally seen in the pages of the California-based magazine, *Arts and Architecture*. In these years he often referred to them as "drawings" although his techniques always began with printer's ink rolled out on a flat surface. In May 1945 five of these "drawings" were reproduced along with a statement by Bertoia referring to a book of eighty-four from which the five had been selected. In that statement he said, "Those here reproduced are from this book which itself is the result of many previous attempts. As varied as the ap-

proaches have been, so the results. While doing them, my whole being functioned through time, analogous to a bird or a frog giving audible form to its song or croak—as you please. . . . The path of action becomes important, the scribbled page becomes something like a by-product. The result rather than the aim suggests book form."[19]

If the eighty-four drawings were actually reproduced as a book, the whereabouts of such a book is not now known. However, there is still in existence today ample evidence of Bertoia's intention to group his graphic works of this period in sequence and present them in book format. Before he was married, on the occasion of the forty-sixth birthday of his mother-in-law to be, he presented Mrs. Valentiner with a sheaf of twenty-five tiny (5⅛ by 6⅞ inches each), colorful monographics that he labeled on a covering sheet as "Graphic Poem" and signed, "HB 1943." Another group of sixty-seven, slightly larger in size and all of a distinctly linear nature, were gathered together in April 1945 with the following note appended in Bertoia's handwriting:

This was done in three colors and black. Black was then changed into dark purple when another color, green came into play. These pages should be kept as they are now arranged and where one begins to look makes no difference. Either No. 67 or No. 1 could be the beginning.

Purity of color and recurrence of motif are indicative of its simple structure and its limitations. They don't vie for significance, although significance there is and they don't pretend to be anything but what they are.[20]

On July 8, 1946, his friend Oskar Fischinger photographed on slide film a series of one hundred thirty-four of Bertoia's prints that demonstrates cohesiveness of continuity along with remarkable variety. While the original graphics seem to exist no longer as a set, the slides are preserved in the Fischinger Archive in California.

Many years later, in 1978, shortly before his death, Bertoia arranged for private publication of a series called *Fifty Drawings*, which he had been saving since 1943.[21] This beautiful publication, copyrighted in 1980 by the Estate of Harry Bertoia, was designed by Quentin Fiore, a friend, and consists of five-hundred numbered copies. Other than the fifty full-size, single-page reproductions, it contains only two short printed statements. One of these is a summation of Bertoia's thoughts about his life in relation to his art. The other explains the origin of these particular works as well as some of the techniques used in their production. Both statements will be discussed later.

The retention of these California monographics of 1943 as a group for thirty-five years marks the beginning of Bertoia's realization of their importance as a significant body of his work. He became more reluctant to release them except, of course, those promised to and sold through the Nierendorf Gallery. After the end of that relationship in 1947, only occasionally did he give any to a gallery for exhibition. When he did so, he placed higher and higher insurance values on them and frequently specified that they were not for sale.

As time went on, the graphics were increasingly cherished by Bertoia, and he was often torn between his innate generosity and his desire to preserve them. For instance, in a letter to Kaare Berntsen of the KB Galleri in Oslo in 1977, he wrote, "I have added six more graphics as you have requested. If you wish to reduce the insurance value [Berntsen thought five-thousand dollars each was too high and had suggested five-hundred dollars] . . . that would be acceptable, however, I value these graphics highly. They have become irreplaceable."[22] When a fire destroyed the storeroom of the Heinie-Onstad Museum in Høvikodden, Norway, in September 1978, Bertoia wrote giving up-to-date values on two large sculptures that had been stored there and added, "I hope the graphics have not been destroyed. Such a loss would indeed be painful as both Brigitta and I love them."[23] Twelve monographics went up in smoke in that fire.

The importance of the graphics to Bertoia did not lie in a narcissistic admiration for his own work but rather in his recognition of their aesthetic value. In addition, they formed a record of his thoughts and ideas. They were

from the beginning, and remained throughout his career, the source for all his work.

All were the result of leisure-time activity, as Bertoia was continually employed one way or another throughout the decade. From 1947 on, part of his leisure was devoted to his early experiments with sculpture, and he also continued to produce jewelry from time to time. For these activities he rented a small, fenced-in space in what had been a gigantic aircraft factory. His earliest sculptures often consisted of a single vertical rod anchored in a flat base, rising high to support a carefully balanced curved rod or other appendage.[24] The use of rods in his sculpture no doubt evolved from their use as chair supports. However, many of the monographics of the 1940s reveal an early interest in strong verticals with balancing forms at their tops, and the linear quality of the drawings is reflected also in those early sculptures.

In addition to these other pursuits, from 1947 to 1949 he was planning, with the cooperation of Harry Weese from Chicago by mail, to build a small modern house of collaborative design (at a cost of nine-thousand dollars) on some property he had purchased in Pacific Palisades. Originally it was to include a separate shop and studio, but to trim costs these were reduced on the plans to a "graphics room" to be equipped to Bertoia's specifications. The house was never built—a result, no doubt, of the move to Pennsylvania in 1950—but letters and plans mailed back and forth across half a continent must have occupied a considerable portion of Bertoia's time.

The Move to Pennsylvania (the 1950s)

When Hans and Florence Knoll made an offer to Bertoia that included the possibility of his designing his own group of furniture, he was urged by his wife to accept, even though his acceptance necessitated moving to eastern Pennsylvania where the Knoll factory was located. The family (including two children) moved from California in the summer of 1950 and in October leased a house in New Hope, a delightful old Bucks County town along the Delaware River with a canal and tow path from Colonial times and a fairly good-sized artists' colony (in summer it is still a tourist Mecca). They lived there for a year but, especially in winter, the more-than-one-hour commute to the Knoll workshop became burdensome.

Bertoia decided to move his family closer to Pennsburg, where the Knoll factory is located, and in June 1952 he leased—and later bought—the two-hundred-year-old fieldstone farmhouse near Barto, complete with pond and barn and some surrounding acreage, where he remained for the rest of his days. He used the barn for a studio, where he worked on both graphics and sculpture during his free time.

During the first two years in Pennsylvania, his main energies went into working out the design problems involved in producing a new line of furniture.[25] The diamond-shaped chair made of metal rods was introduced by Knoll in December 1952 and, along with its affiliated pieces, became part of what is known as the "Bertoia Collection."[26] When the collection was first brought out, it was exhibited in Knoll showrooms along with some of the small sculptures Bertoia had been producing since 1947. While some of the sculptures continued the linear verticals of the California monographics, a number of them adapted the motif of repetitive geometric forms that had also originated in his prints. They were translations into actuality of the three-dimensional aspects of his early graphics.[27]

Bertoia was given his first major commission for a large-scale sculpture by his friend, the Yale- and Cranbrook-trained architect Eero Saarinen. It was completed in 1953.[28] It was then that he acquired a new studio in what had been the Knoll metal shop in the nearby town of Bally, severed his relationship as a Knoll employee, and began devoting himself in earnest to sculpture. He maintained a friendly relationship with Knoll throughout the rest of his life, however, and his sculptures and occasionally his graphics were often exhibited in Knoll showrooms all over the world.[29] Beginning with the welded-metal screen for Saarinen's General Motors Technical Center, commission after commission followed with increasing momentum.

In view of his preoccupation in the early fifties with design problems and, later, with sculpture commissions, Bertoia's production of graphics during this decade was somewhat sporadic. Very few were done between 1950 and 1952; there was considerable activity between 1952 and 1956; and a resurgence after 1957 carried over into the early sixties. As it turned out, in spite of the intermittent nature of his attention to printmaking, more monographics were produced in the 1950s than in any other decade of his career. He worked on them at home for relaxation at night. In his Bally studio during the daytime, they were done often to work out ideas for sculpture. He used them to solve problems of design, scale, and cutting of sheet metal. Notations often indicate metalworking methods or clarify structural ideas. Monographics were sometimes submitted as proposals to prospective clients, and at times they were made after the fact as a record of a work completed and delivered. While some of the graphics were exhibited occasionally along with his sculptures at Fairweather Hardin Gallery in Chicago, which began representing him as early as 1955, and at Staempfli Gallery in New York in the 1960s, most were retained in his growing collection.

The year 1957 was something of a watershed for Bertoia. After his successes of the early fifties with sculpture commissions and a craftsmanship medal received in 1956 from the American Institute of Architects, he was awarded a ten-thousand-dollar fellowship by the Graham Foundation for Advanced Studies in the Fine Arts, a Chicago-based philanthropic organization. Among other things, this permitted him to take a six weeks' hiatus in the form of a spring trip to Italy, his first since emigration in 1930.

During this trip he visited family in Udine, as well as the art-historical sights of Rome, Florence, and Venice for the first time. It was a time for contemplation, for standing back and "observing in silence," prior to regeneration.[30] And the regeneration of his monographics in the late fifties shows some new directions.

Sculpture Dominates (the 1960s)

Considerably fewer monographics were produced by Bertoia during the 1960s. There were several reasons for this. Most importantly, the number of sculpture commissions increased tremendously, many of them for works of gigantic size and considerable intricacy. For some, such as the Dulles Airport bronze of 1962, the preparation time was extensive although the actual production time was not.[31] For others, sometimes as much as six months to a year of actual cutting, brazing, and welding of the metal components was necessary for completion of a single project. During the sixties there were twenty-one large commissions, each involving travel first for consultations with architects and patrons and later to oversee installations.[32] This compares with only thirteen similar commissions during the previous decade.

In addition, Bertoia prepared for many special exhibitions of his smaller sculptures held frequently during the decade by his New York and Chicago galleries and in Knoll showrooms in various cities of the United States as well as in Buenos Aires, Paris, Amsterdam, Zurich, Milan, Rome, and four cities in Germany. There was also an exhibition in London in 1963, in which he participated.[33] He traveled to Europe several times during the sixties to be present for openings. Each of the exhibitions entailed a considerable amount of paperwork, preparation, and crating, not to mention the design and completion of the sculptures involved. In spite of his taking on two employees to help with some of the mundane tasks in the studio, there was simply less time available for Bertoia's favorite form of relaxation, his graphics.

In the sixties Bertoia began to have another preoccupation, one that became almost an obsession. This was his interest in making music from the sounds of his sculptures. Since his earliest metal works with their tall stems and precarious balance, Bertoia's sculptures had involved movement. And when metal pieces move and touch each other, sounds are emitted, different sounds from different metals. A reviewer of one of the early sculpture exhibitions wrote in 1953: "Some of the sculpture can be taken apart and swings, much of it shivers, most of it rings with different tones if you flick your fingernail at it, and even the most rigid 'Multiplane Constructions' vibrate."[34]

The materials used by Bertoia for his sculptures were ordered from industrial metal suppliers. Whenever a large shipment of rods and wires was delivered to his studio, it was accompanied by the music of the clanging metals. As work proceeded with different rods gripped in a vise for brazing, welding, or polishing, an occasional twang would occur as metal struck metal inadvertently. These sounds intrigued the sculptor and he resolved to investigate further.

About 1960, Bertoia began constructing sculptures of identical vertical rods welded in rows on a flat metal platform. From piece to piece he varied the length of the rods, their number, diameter, and the kind of metal used. Sometimes he would weld different metals to the tops of the rods, like cylindrical caps. He began in this way to experiment with the tonal variety which could be obtained as one flexible strand was plucked to set in motion all the rest or the entire group of rods in one sculpture was vigorously rubbed together. In the first case a bell-like sound was achieved; in the second, a soft whir or a dramatic clang. In 1964 Clifford West, a filmmaker and Bertoia's friend since Cranbrook days, made a film (released the following year) about Bertoia's sculpture. The background music for the film was derived from the sculptures themselves.[35]

By 1966 Bertoia was intrigued enough to order over a thousand pounds of beryllium-copper rods in many different diameters and lengths so that he could construct enough sculptures to produce a variety of sounds.[36] By the end of the decade, he had interested his brother Oreste, who had considerable musical talent, in the project. It had become so extensive by this time that in 1968–69 it required the remodeling of the barn on his home property to act as a sounding board for the sculpture-instruments placed there. It was at this time, also, that an extensive cabinetry system of drawers was established on the upper level of the barn studio to house his collection of monographics.

Obviously, all these activities reduced the amount of time Bertoia had to give to his drawings in the sixties. Nevertheless, a sufficient number of them exists to enable us to trace new ideas and developments of old ones. Some of the prints of the late sixties are closely related to, and difficult to distinguish from, those of the early seventies. It may well be, therefore, that some of those discussed under the latter group belong to the former.

The Last Years (1970–78)

In spite of the fact that Bertoia lived only until 1978 and was ill for a good part of the last year of his life, there was a considerable increase during the seventies in the number of his monographics. Architectural sculpture commissions decreased from twenty-one in the sixties to slightly more than half that number, but the number of one-man shows and other special exhibitions increased. And there was an enormous increase in travel, much of it foreign travel. For example, exhibitions of his work were held at several different locations in Norway and Denmark during the seventies, and Bertoia went to Oslo and Bergen for openings in 1972, 1976, and in May 1978. He was also present in Caracas for the opening of a one-man exhibition in March 1977, at which time he was prevailed upon to speak to the architecture students of the University of Venezuela.[37] In January 1976 he made an extended trip, in part to visit the pre-Columbian sites of Machu Picchu (a long-cherished dream fulfilled), Guatemala, and the Yucatan, but also to visit Knoll showrooms en route.

These trips were in addition to those for consultations and installations within the continental United States. The year 1975 was a particularly busy one with three major commissions to complete and four exhibitions.

Most surprisingly, at the urging of gallery owner Kaare Berntsen in Norway, Bertoia even returned briefly in the seventies to designing jewelry, this time for casting in gold.[38] The last time he had designed and made small works for personal adornment was in 1948 and 1949 when he produced a number of necklaces, bracelets, pins, and earrings in silver and in ebony and nylon for Cranbrook friends to sell in specialty shops in Chicago and Boston.[39] When the Museum of Modern Art wrote in 1966, asking to exhibit some of his jewelry, his reply indicated that there was none available.[40] He sent photographs instead.

The "musical program," as he called it, also continued to occupy a great deal of Bertoia's time during these last years. Since 1969, the remodeled barn on his home property had been its site. Seventy-five or more sculptures were installed on the raised and reinforced wood floor representing many different sizes and tonalities of the standing beryllium-copper-rod pieces as well as sculptures made of flexible sheafs of stainless-steel wire. New pieces were brought in from time to time in the search for new sounds. Suspended from the ceiling were several gongs and grouped metal bars that clanged together when touched. Bertoia worked with the instruments daily and whenever his brother Oreste could come from Detroit to join him, the two of them made recordings of their performances and critically analyzed the tapes.[41]

By mid-1971 there were several hundred tapes, and the two men must have become interested in bettering conditions in the barn because Bertoia sought outside help. In a letter to the Rockefeller Foundation he described the work done so far, mentioned the "vast potential for further development of this unfolding musical form," and went on to say, "I would want to develop a round container in the form of a building acoustically satisfying the requirements of the factors involved."[42] Either the letter was never sent or the request was turned down, for the circular structure was never built.

In November 1970 some of the tapes were put together and a twelve-inch long-playing record was made bearing the jacket label and disc label *Sonambient,* an obvious reference to a "sound environment" and a name Bertoia had devised for the music of his tonal sculptures. Through legal steps this became a registered trademark in 1972.[43] The performance on side 1 was entitled "Bellissima, Bellissima, Bellissima"; that on side 2 was called "Nova." At least eight more recordings based on the tapes were issued after 1978 by Bertoia's widow, all labeled *Sonambient* and with equally evocative performance titles.[44]

In 1971, at the instigation of a young producer, a film was made entitled *Sonambients: The Sound Sculpture of Harry Bertoia,* in which the barn was the setting and the instruments supplied the sound track.[45] In it, Bertoia is seen talking about and "playing" the sculptures. Later he made the following statements concerning his interest in sounds to a reporter from Chicago:

Everything has its own sound, and my idea is to try to get away from the tonal scale to explore some of the many other relationships. . . .

At the start . . . I was curious to speed ahead and produce as many sounds as possible. But then I listened for what was not here, and it is *that* I still want to find. I began on my own initiative, then heard references. So I bought a few records—Edgar Varese, John Cage—and evaluated what they had done. My basic intent, tho [sic], is to develop something with its own energy. If it is good, it will continue; if not, it will fade away, as it should."[46]

By October 1977 the first signs of bronchial cancer—a disease probably brought on by his failure to use a mask when welding beryllium copper—had become apparent. Bertoia had lost his voice and was concerned enough about his health to visit a doctor and have some tests made. According to the "diagnosis," which his son Val gave to a friend, they proved negative.[47] He did not regain his voice until sometime in March 1978 after visiting a Philadelphia throat specialist recommended by the owners of his Chicago gallery as a result of their concern.[48] His travels that year included the Bahamas in January for his health; Norway in May; Colorado in June to visit one of his daughters; Richmond, Virginia in July for an installation (his last); and California in late September from which point another daughter took him to Mexico for treatment, returning to Pennsylvania in mid-October. He continued to work whenever he was at home completing commissions and shipping pieces for exhibition to both his Chicago and New York galleries.[49]

By September his health had deteriorated drastically. On September 5 he learned by means of a cable that a storeroom had burned down in Norway, destroying two of his sculptures and twelve graphics. It is in his subsequent letters to Kaare Berntsen in Oslo, at whose home he had stayed that spring, that it is possible to follow his progress in his own words:

[September 18] I have not had a chance to do work on the jewelry as there is much paper work to be organized. I feel the compression of time and the last visit to the doctor was not encouraging.[50]

[October 20] I should try to bring you up to date on my state of health. My physical energies are diminishing every day. I have reached the point where my activities are reduced drastically. One or two hours of movement. Then I find it difficult to breathe and I have to rest which means many hours in bed. My appetite is poor and I have lost much weight, 40 lbs. or more. . . . Strange, but I have a feeling that every letter might turn out to be the last one. Please take good care of yourself and your dear family and enjoy life as much as you can.[51]

Berntsen came to the United States a few days in advance of the November 9 opening of the Munch exhibition at the National Gallery in Washington that year. He wrote asking if he could come to see Bertoia, who cabled back: "Yes if you can come visit me anytime convenient for you from November 3 to November 6 I would be happy and looking forward to seeing you."[52] Berntsen and Clifford West visited with him the evening of November 5. On November 6, 1978, at 5:30 P.M., Harry Bertoia died of a pulmonary hemorrhage brought on by "massively metastasized bronchogenic carcinoma."[53]

Nearly a month earlier, on October 9, the following words of Bertoia's, spoken to Dr. Franco Toso and Winfred Brueggemann, were noted down by them and sent to Mrs. Bertoia after her husband's death:

My dear friends, I must tell you something important. Man has no choice as to when and where he is born, but he has some choice as to when and how he dies. Although I do appreciate the good intentions you all have for me, a man understands when his time has come, and nothing in the world can change this fact of life. I wish I could stay. But I accept this fact of life as truth and I have no regrets. I had a beautiful life and I am not afraid. Man is not important. Humanity is what counts, to which I feel I have given my contribution. Humanity shall continue without me, but I am not going away—I am not leaving you. Every time you see some treetops moving in the wind, you will think of me, or if you see some beautiful flower—you will think of me. I have never been a very religious man, not in the formal way, but each time I took a walk in the woods—I felt the presence of a superior force around me. I thank you all for your good intentions.[54]

3. Tools and Techniques

Bertoia's printing techniques were from the first experimental. He began by working in the print shop at Cranbrook at night after his daytime duties teaching metalworking. His first graphics in 1938–39 were woodcuts of a traditional nature, but he soon became bored with them. To hear him tell it in his own words many years later, "I was doing wood cuts, carving on a piece of wood then printing. I needed a press for that. After doing a little bit of that I got tired because one print after another came out identical. I said: oh this won't do. I got the notion that if I cut that block of wood in many parts then I could change the parts and there would be something new coming out. So that really happened. And I was delighted. I said, oh, this is fun."[1] The result was the geometric prints that were hand stamped through "the use of a small block of wood, pressed on paper repeatedly" (plates 1, 2, and 3).[2] Many variations ensued, first changes of geometric form, then the addition of line to the surface of the print, and eventually arrangements of a variety of forms in a single composition (plates 4, 5, and 6). Bertoia's use of this, the earliest original technique he developed, was discontinued during the 1950s after a few variations on the theme tying the technique closely to his sculpture screens of the period.

A tactile quality was introduced at first through thickly applied inks and oil colors. Later, variations in texture were obtained through the contrast of transparency and opacity and the adoption of new tools and methods to help secure these properties.

The linear works and those combining form with line used entirely different techniques. Both the dark-field and light-field methods of monotype were employed by Bertoia during the 1940s (plates 7 through 10), often combined with additional printing techniques (plate 20, among others). In the sixties he returned to the monotype for a graphic that reflects the unusual method developed by Bertoia for its sculptural realization. Plate 61 is not a line drawing but a painted monotype showing considerable evidence of having been worked directly on the plate with wiping and scratching. It had to be handled speedily before the ink became too dry for printing, much as the molten bronze of the panels for which this graphic was made had to be worked in a matter of minutes before it hardened. This return to the true monotype technique was not prophetic, however, as nothing similar to it appeared again.

Instead, Bertoia evolved early in his first decade of working with monographics a printing procedure that suited him and that he continued to use for the rest of his life. What he wrote about it in the statement accompanying his book, *Fifty Drawings*, referred to in chapter 2, is of considerable interest to this study:

Thirty-five years ago in a small beach house by the Pacific Ocean on the coast of California, this book began to take its form. It was my intent to explore a technical means that would permit me to work with great rapidity. I had done a considerable amount of experimentation with materials that were on hand and processes that would evolve in the course of action. All this points to a technical development needed to permit the fluidity of thought to evolve from page to page without disruption or discontinuity. Speed of execution being essential, it became possible by drawing on the back side of the paper using fingers, thumb, palm and various tools made of wood or metal. The ink was rolled on glass. Pressure picked up the ink in a granular way, which I liked. Drawing on the back side of the page did not permit clear visibility, a great advantage, for it necessitated inner vision to take over the function of the eye. Surprises were always in store when the paper was turned over. Traces of the image would register on the next page which initiated a play of dark and light line and tone.

Technique and image were developing along parallel lines, interacting and transmogrifying no end.

The whole sequence of fifty pages came into being, in about twenty-four hours of uninterrupted work.[3]

Thirty-four of the fifty drawings are linear, while the others combine form with line. None of them exhibits any of the geometric rigidities and repetitions of his strictly formal works. There is a considerable variety of both form and line, the latter ranging from the most delicate curvilinear tracings against soft, almost vaporous backgrounds to strong, dark, straight lines shadowed by ghostly whites against a granular dark ground. Those containing form show no recognizable objects, but rather many irregular shapes floating in space, both negative and positive, both dark and light, often connected by, or associated with, meandering line. All are monochromatic and were accomplished by means of printer's ink using a variety of implements.

The result is as intriguing as the technique. It can be seen changing and bringing about new images from plate to plate as a particular motif is worked out. Sometimes the result is amusing. In one print a single egg shape dominates the center surrounded by a light aura from which curved lines, both dark and light, sweep into the surrounding blackness. In the next the ovoid sphere is replaced by four circular forms of differing sizes, two of which are black, one smaller and white, and the last—smallest of all—a scribble of circular black lines. Each is surrounded by its own light halo, and the forms are connected by gracefully looping lines, some of which are black, shadowed by white "ghosts," and some are simply white, or negative, against the positive dark background.

In another print the line is first negative, then positive, tracing undulating form against a dark ground until line, form, and space become indistinguishable one from the other as positive and negative interact, changing place before one's eyes. In yet another, a single curving line retraces and overlaps itself in ever widening protrusions until the bent head of a figure holding a child seems to emerge—a highly abstracted Madonna. Several of the "drawings" include cognates (negative images of the previous print) and are obviously part of a miniseries within the larger group of fifty.

The statement on technique accompanying the fifty drawings indicates the reason for the development by Bertoia of his unique working method—"speed of execution." Another time, in speaking of making the graphics he said, "I had to be speedy because I wanted to be ahead of my thought. If I could only stay within my inner self and work fast so that reason and awareness would not come in yet, then it would be fine."[4] Obviously a kind of automatic transference was sought. We are reminded that the fifty drawings (and, one assumes, additional rejected ones) were done in one twenty-four-hour period. This conjures up a vivid picture of "genius at work" oblivious to all save his art, tossing off page after page in a sustained concentration of effort brought on by inspiration. Such a romantic image is considerably dispelled by his claim, with regard to his sculpture at least, that he did it "by working like hell." "I don't think there is such a thing," he continued, "as a moment of inspiration."[5] Clearly, however, he achieved in California in the forties his avowed aim of finding a technique that would permit him to "work with great rapidity" and spontaneity.

The method described became standard operating procedure for Bertoia, whether for works intended as compositions of aesthetic merit or for working drawings of a strictly practical nature. He did make direct sketches from time to time for record keeping of works out on consignment or exhibition and, occasionally, for patrons who insisted upon authentication of his unsigned sculptures. However, such sketches are invariably small and quite summary in nature with a minimum of detail and no shading, in blue or black ink on ordinary typewriter paper. They are usually accompanied by a notation concerning measurements and materials.

His preferred method involved inking a glass or smooth Masonite plate, then placing the paper on top and drawing from the back with implements which made no mark on the back of the paper. A granular effect was achieved in broad irregular sweeps by the use of the side or the palm of his hand or a clean brayer rolled lightly across the back of the paper. Smaller areas of granular shading came from the heel of the hand, the thumb, or a finger. Lines were produced ranging from hair-fine to finger-thick with many different implements: a rounded metal stylus; balsa-wood sticks of various thicknesses, beveled and used flatly against the surface (plates 40 and 41); a wire dog brush which produced multitudinous fine lines with a single stroke (plates 53 to 58); and even, in some works from the 1950s not illustrated here, Bertoia's own hand and foot prints built up in overlapping layers of black and colored inks. The latter method produced some attractive prints but was a gimmick that did not last. Once adopted, other new tools continued to be of service, however, each to produce its own particular desired degree of softness, hardness, or delicacy of touch.

The wire brush responsible for many striated effects can be seen at the upper left in figure 1. The photograph

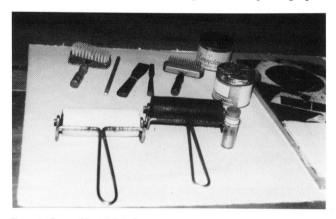

Figure 1. Some of Bertoia's tools.

displays some of the tools still to be found in Bertoia's studio at this writing, including several brayers (one hard and heavily inked, the other uninked and of soft rubber), spatula, palette knife, broad stick, and pots of ink. The soft rubber brayer was probably used on the back of the paper for printing, and a simple wooden board such as that at the right in the photograph was used for rolling out the ink. These, plus his hands (figure 2) were the

basic tools used throughout the years by Bertoia for his monographics.

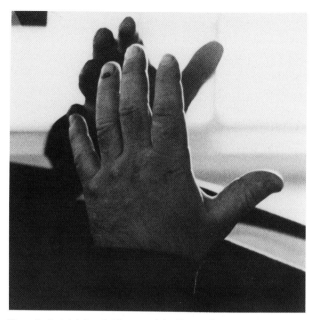

Figure 2. Bertoia's hands. Photograph by George Cserna.

In many works the technique of ''shadowing'' is used —dark lines are followed exactly by white ones a hair's breadth to one side. This might have been accomplished by lifting the paper after the drawing was completed and replacing it just slightly to one side before printing with hand or brayer pressure. Or it is possible that it is an inadvertent result of rolling the back of the paper with a brayer, causing the paper to move slightly in the process. This type of ''accident'' could have been one of the surprises that were such a delight to Bertoia when he pulled each print.

The translucency of rice paper was important also, allowing, as it did, for limited visibility in the pursuit of a particular image so that much of the work had to be intuitive. Knowing when to stop became crucial, particularly in view of Bertoia's desire to leave something to the imagination, not to state it all. The element of chance was always there and, in fact, as is indicated in his statement, this was what made it exciting enough to continue to hold his interest. Adaptation of the "happy accident" contributes to the success of many of the monographics throughout the decades.

What takes his preferred technique out of the category of simple transfer drawing is Bertoia's frequent reuse of the negative afterimage of a previous print. The use of a cognate in the process Bertoia developed produces a different effect from such use in the usual process of printing. In the traditional monotype method, the artist paints or draws directly on a metal plate, which is printed on wet paper under heavy pressure such as only a press can give. Where there is ink or oil paint on the plate most of it is transferred to the paper. Where there is none, either because none was put there or because it was wiped or scratched away, the paper remains white. The cognate, or second printing, of such a plate repeats the first plate exactly, only much paler and with whatever changes the artist cares to make prior to the second printing.

With Bertoia's method of drawing from the back of the paper which has been laid over an inked glass plate, each line or smudge that is drawn removes ink from rather than places ink on the glass. Therefore, when a cognate is made, it comes up the exact reverse in line and tone of the previous print. Where a line or a form is inked on the first print, it will be white on the second and on any succeeding prints. Even if the artist reinks the glass and works directly on its surface before reprinting (as Bertoia has done with plate 8), he will get light lines and forms where he formerly had dark ones and vice versa in areas of the plate that have not been reworked (upper left in plate 8). The printing is done only with hand or brayer pressure, never by using a press.

Plate 10 is a cognate exhibiting some of the traits of both processes. The original, plate 9, shows evidence of drawing directly on the glass before the paper was laid

over it. The dark, central figure, particularly, shows white lines that were scratched out of dark ink as well as dark lines drawn from the back of the paper after it had been laid on the plate (figure 3). The same white lines in this

Figure 3. Detail of plate 9.

area of the cognate, plate 10 (figure 4), are still white, but they appear much less bright as the ridges of ink which surrounded them were lifted off the glass with the first

Figure 4. Detail of plate 10.

printing. The lines drawn from the back of the paper, dark in the first print, become white in the second. Any of the areas rubbed from behind are dark in the first print, whereas in the second print these are light, and the surrounding areas dark.

This intriguing play of negative and positive is seen used in many different ways. Plates 13 and 14 are especially notable for their adaptation of cognates to new developments. Four more pairs of cognate prints (plates 34 and 35, 49 and 50, 54 and 55, and 56 and 57) point up in different degrees the varied results obtainable in the shift from positive to negative values. In addition, the use of a common cognate in plates 38 and 52 illustrates the capacity of such adaptation to produce graphics of widely differing style and content. The adaptation of afterimages to a totally new composition is nowhere more beautifully demonstrated than in plate 38, a print with possible practical application to sculpture. This technique is used frequently in both sculpture studies and works of pure aesthetic purpose. In the latter it enhances the dreamlike quality of fantasy and in the former it helps make a work of art out of what might otherwise be just a working drawing.

The technique of drawing on the back of the paper somewhat resembles the method Gauguin used for his so-called traced monotypes, printed drawings, or transfer drawings.[6] However, in Bertoia's works there is no original pencil drawing retained on the verso. This, plus the fact that more often than not, his technique is combined with drawing on the glass, scratching, wiping, paper-surface additions, and, frequently, the use of a cognate, leads to considerable complexity indeed and puts these graphics more clearly in the realm of experimental works.

Bertoia's monographics are the result of a combination of drawing methods hand-printed, either from repeated woodblocks or through the use of a glass plate, a brayer, and hand pressure. Like many other artists who have taken up the medium, he was never taught any monotype processes. Consequently, his tools and procedures were innovative. It is often extremely difficult to determine exactly how a particular effect was achieved.[7] Their complexity is what intrigues but it often takes these prints out of the category of "pure monotype." Considered as monographics, however, they rival the best in modern experimental printmaking.

4. Analysis

Monographics and Sculpture

From the comprehensive selection of prints displayed here, it should be apparent that the complete graphics of Harry Bertoia represent a body of work as considerable as that of his sculptures. A lifelong (thirty-eight working years) experimentation with various techniques for making monographics, many of them variations on the monotype process, each of them unique (never reproduced in an edition), resulted in an oeuvre of unprecedented proportions in the field of printmaking. As stated in the preface of *The Painterly Print,* "The fact that monotypes are unique prints rather than multiples accounts for both their scarcity and their relative obscurity. Until recently so few artists produced monotypes that they were considered curiosities, even among knowledgeable print collectors and connoisseurs. . . . Not until 1968 was substantial interest in monotypes developed."[1]

Bertoia began working with monotypes in 1940, nearly a decade before his first attempts in the three-dimensional area. He continued producing them along with other monographics throughout his career as an internationally renowned designer and metal sculptor. With regard to his work in both media, as early as 1958 he said, "In the metal I have to go slowly and deliberately; it is difficult to make changes and I try to avoid them. In graphics it is really the opposite. It's like a dream: it goes fast, lines, planes, smudges, throwing ink—it becomes a kind of somnambulistic medium."[2]

In 1961 he wrote out a brief statement that gives us further insight into the interrelationships in his work:

Metals and graphics have held an equal interest for me. Metals require thought and deliberate action. Some can hold a precise dimension, others prefer to be worked in a molten state, still others are elastic, and these and many other characteristics are the complement to graphics.

The graphic medium is more spontaneous, responds to the touch with immediacy, is less demanding of reason, and widens horizons to the imagination.

To do one, then the other, is refreshing and stimulating, and one medium can do what the other could not. Yet at times they merge into a single image.[3]

Bertoia was not particularly interested in astrology but his wife, he said, informed him that he was a Pisces, born under the water sign of two fish swimming in opposite directions. He likened his work in metals and graphics to the two fish because they are "almost opposite in their approach," the one speedy and almost dreaming, the other necessitating measurements and calculations, allowing little chance for the subconscious to operate.[4]

In many ways Bertoia's graphics are reflected in his sculptures. The vertical balance of his earliest metal works, the geometric precision of the screens of the fifties, the spherical forms made up of radiating rods, all are seen first in the paper works of the forties. Clearly, the graphics represented a major source for the sculpture. Here was where the artist felt most free to explore and invent.

Sometimes, especially during the sixties when Bertoia was at the height of his career as a sculptor, the reflection reverses itself: the graphics are affected by the three-dimensional medium. Their images take on more substance and are often closely related, in the nature of working drawings, to specific sculpture commissions. Throughout the decades, however, the graphics were the repository for all that was most inventive and experimental in Bertoia's aesthetic consciousness with regard to ideas, impressions, forms, and techniques. They deserve to be considered on their own merit as a separate phase of his life's work, however inextricably they may be bound to his sculpture.

The Influences

Before summarizing and discussing the accomplishments

of the monographics, it behooves us to investigate the influences on that work.

His admiration for and attachment to his brother Oreste, six years his senior and an accomplished amateur musician, was certainly a factor in Bertoia's early lyrical monotypes as well as in his lifelong interest in the sounds of his sculpture. More importantly, it was Oreste—himself unlettered—who counseled his fifteen-year-old younger brother to go to school rather than take a job when he first arrived in Detroit. It was his schooling at Cass Technical High School that led him, through scholarships, to the Cranbrook Academy of Art and his career.

At Cranbrook he was enrolled to study drawing and painting, not sculpture. Certainly, the freedom accorded students and faculty at this institution in its early years was an important factor in Bertoia's developing his experimental approach. It was here that he first learned of the Bauhaus, its methods and something of the results of those methods. And the occasional direct contact with a visiting modern architect such as Walter Gropius was a powerful stimulant to his already strong creative urge. Added to the everyday give-and-take among colleagues, such special attractions helped make life at Cranbrook an aesthetic experience. It was a stimulating atmosphere in which to work.

However, neither the resident sculptor, Carl Milles, nor the head of the painting department, Zoltan Sepeshy, revealed in their work any acceptance of the early twentieth-century innovation of nonobjectivity. In fact, little of the more experimental work could be seen first hand at Cranbrook. The most ambitious exhibition held there during Bertoia's tenure celebrated, in 1940, the works of the U.S. realist painters of the thirties.[5]

Bertoia's nonobjective work was self-generated, although doubtless not without occasional stimulus from other artists whose work he admired. Such stimulus in his early years—the years 1939–41 when he was formulating his style and techniques in the print medium—was

probably limited to the reproductions and discussions in the art magazines available at Cranbrook. It is interesting to note that from September 1937 to the end of 1938, a series of "how-to" articles on the various graphics processes (including monotype) appeared in *Art Instruction*, a magazine to which the first-time teacher was likely to have turned for aid and comfort. They may very well have been the impetus for Bertoia's first forays into the print shop.

Reproductions of nonrepresentational work in the art periodicals of the time were sparse in those years, though the pace began to pick up somewhat in 1940–41. Whether or not Bertoia got to see the loan exhibition from the Guggenheim Foundation of originals by Kandinsky, Klee, Mondrian, and others, which was displayed at the Women's City Club in Detroit in May 1942, is problematical.[6] In any case, by this time he had other sources of inspiration in the works by European artists owned by his future father-in-law. It is clear that Bertoia's association, beginning in 1941, with Dr. William R. Valentiner, director of the Detroit Institute of Arts from 1924 to 1945, was a revelation to him. Dr. Valentiner, a Rembrandt scholar, was one of the first art historians in the United States to understand and collect, both personally and for the institute, the German expressionist painters. His personal collection, which Bertoia came to know well, included drawings and paintings by Kirchner, Schmidt-Rottluff, Nolde, Kandinsky, and multiple works by Klee.[7]

But expressionism was not what most interested the young Bertoia. Also included among his father-in-law's art works were a painting by Joan Miró and two paintings by Odilon Redon, the French painter of fantastic visions who died in 1916. When the Valentiner collection was divided sometime after his death in 1958, the latter two paintings, entitled *L'Apparition d'une femme nue* and *Dante et Béatrice*, along with a Klee called *Spiral* were acquired by Bertoia from his children. They remained with him until the end of his life. In 1978, when he knew he was dying and with the concurrence of the rest of the family, he gave *L'Apparition* to his nieces, the daughters of his brother Oreste. He wrote, in a letter conveying the painting to its new owners, "I was particularly fond of Redon's work and I made every effort to keep it in the house where we all enjoyed it. . . . I miss it, but I know it is in good hands."[8]

Of Dr. Valentiner's collection, the paintings that appealed most to Bertoia were those of Redon, Klee, and Miró, all artists whose works were often both abstract and objective at the same time,[9] all either associated with, or admired by, members of the surrealist movement of the twenties and thirties. The earliest of the three, Redon, was contemporary with the impressionist painters in France but remained completely aloof from their versions of painted reality. Nature was his inspiration, but he used it as "the logic of the visible at the service of the invisible."[10] Redon is also quoted as saying, "Nothing in art is achieved by will alone. Everything is done by docilely submitting to the arrival of the 'unconscious'."[11] Statements such as these, plus the visual evidence of his graphic fantasies (which he called simply his "blacks"), as well as his later, gloriously colored oil paintings, made his work a precursor to that of André Masson, Max Ernst, and Joan Miró. The latter's work in the twenties and thirties seems at times to combine Redon's visionary motifs with the childlike primitivism and whimsy of Paul Klee.

Klee's *Spiral* that Bertoia kept was the most nonobjective of his works owned by Dr. Valentiner and aptly illustrated Klee's frequently quoted remark about "taking a line for a walk." It is an image of a broad-based double spiral line rising loosely and somewhat asymmetrically through undifferentiated space. It is virtually monochromatic. The Redon *Dante et Béatrice* exhibits two heads emerging from a colorful, vaporous mist. *L'Apparition* consists of a standing nude, the body enveloped in a golden aura, itself surrounded by a larger cloud of pastel tone. At her feet lies a group of brilliantly colored fantastic forms

suggestive of a bouquet. All are small, intimate works presenting lines or forms that appear to float in space. What Bertoia enjoyed about each of these artists, to judge from the carryover into his own work, was their delicacy of touch, flights of fancy, and the general spirit of joyousness that emanated from their more colorful works. In each of them, also, he must have been impressed by the diaphanous textures of the softly merging colors on the painted surfaces of their canvases. Nonrepresentational floating images on softly textured backgrounds became characteristic of Bertoia's work, especially in the 1940s.

His use of geometric figures—the circle, the triangle, the square—may be derived from the constructivists' simplicity of form, as seen in the corner-counter reliefs of Rodchenko and Tatlin and the latter's *Monument to the Third International*. The more irregular shapes and linear meanderings of his graphic works were first used by Bertoia in his jewelry. They may be subconscious reflections of those in the constructions of Naum Gabo and the surrealist paintings of Miró.

That surrealism was a continuing interest of Bertoia is attested by the fact that in 1959, when his association with the Staempfli Gallery in New York was just beginning, he purchased from that organization a Paul Delvaux painting entitled *Paysage aux lanternes* in exchange for several of his own sculptures.[12] Realistically painted, it nevertheless conveyed a sense of mystery. Although he later resold the painting, it was the only time in his life he actually sought to buy the work of another artist.[13]

The avowed definition of surrealism by its early formulators as "a certain psychic automatism that corresponds rather closely to the state of dreaming," their insistence on experimental techniques and the adaptation of the accidental, their spontaneity, all these appealed to Bertoia.[14] As he said of his technique, he preferred working from the back of the paper "for it necessitated inner vision to take over the function of the eye." In another statement, written in 1976, he was even more explicit about his debt to surrealism when he referred to "the acceptance of the reality of the dream as a stimulant and propellant toward achieving the other reality."[15]

An artist he admired later in his life was Henri Rousseau ("the *douanier*"), a surrealist forerunner like Redon, whose work at the Museum of Modern Art Bertoia never missed seeing whenever he went to New York. He was especially fond of *The Sleeping Gypsy*, in which he felt that Rousseau "was transferring the very essence of himself. We are not able to prove this in any way. But I feel it is somehow miraculously true. It is not only a question of pigment and placement. There is something more."[16]

Although he did not mention at what stage in his own life he first encountered the twentieth century's most famous artist, Bertoia maintained in 1978 that he had had difficulty. "When I first saw Picasso [his work] I was on the verge of vomiting—not many, only one or two. I stayed away for two or three years until I could approach him again. Now he is my medicine. It's a tonic. It's the novelty of the exposure to which we react strongly."[17]

Well before 1943 when he left Cranbrook, Bertoia had firmly established nonobjective imagery in his graphic works. His friendship in California from 1943 to 1950 with Oskar Fischinger, painter and maker of nonrepresentational films, was no doubt another strengthening factor. Fischinger had begun in Germany about 1920 by graphically analyzing poetry—its moods and dramatic development—in lines of strength or delicacy on long, horizontal sheets of drawing paper. From this he progressed to animations on film in the twenties and early thirties, synchronizing the nonobjective images to music. In such films the dynamics of motion and sound were explored in line and geometric figure, and eventually also in color. In Hollywood, from 1936, Fischinger worked with Disney (on *Fantasia*) and other studios, mostly unhappily, and began painting in a mode not unlike that of his films.[18] When Bertoia met him, at the instigation of Dr. Valentiner and Karl Nierendorf, they had both been protégés of Solomon R. Guggenheim, through the medium of Hilla

Rebay, and both had had exhibitions at the Nierendorf Gallery in New York. Through Nierendorf, who had represented "The Blue Four" in Berlin, they had access in the Los Angeles area to the Galka Scheyer collection of Feininger, Jawlensky, Kandinsky, and Klee that later went to the Norton Simon Museum in Pasadena. The similarity in Bertoia's and Fischinger's work of image and aesthetic, which each had developed independently, led to mutual admiration and a friendship that outlasted the days of their geographical proximity.[19] It also led to such coincidences as Fischinger's naming a 1938 film *An Optical Poem,* of which Bertoia was completely unaware when, before he left Michigan in 1943, he devised the phrase "Graphic Poem" for his works in series.

Bertoia's nonobjective style developed far from the New York City of the abstract expressionists in the 1940s. Even in the fifties, when he had moved to within seventy-five miles of New York, he eschewed contact with the by now thriving artistic community in that city. "I prefer working in relative isolation in a place like Bally. I think artists who congregate in New York tend to excite each other too much. They begin to respond more to what others are doing or saying than to the vision within," he said in 1975.[20] Instead, he found both life and work wonderful in the country.

The introduction of nature references into his predominantly nonobjective images stemmed at least in part from Bertoia's appreciation of his environment. Frequent remarks, whether from California or Pennsylvania, regarding the exhilaration of being "naked in the surf" or "barefoot in the grass" are testament to the inspiration it gave him. It was never his intention to copy nature, however. Perhaps the closest he came to direct influence was the result of his visit to Ossabaw Island off the coast of Georgia in 1961 at the urging of Eleanor West, founder of its preservation society. He described the island as "almost primeval—wild boars, big oaks, Spanish moss, wide stretches of beach, very few inhabitants."[21] There he watched the sea churning, eroding the land, and became conscious of the constant turmoil of the earth's surface. It was his memory of this experience supplemented by ideas gained from his reading of scientific publications that brought about a series of poured bronze sculptures culminating in the Dulles Airport panels of 1962. He was trying to capture the very process of evolution.

If Bertoia's imagination was titillated by the minutiae of pine needles glistening in the sunlight after rain or a flower petal curving gracefully in a hyperbolic parabola, it was also intrigued by the immensity of the universe. The sky, the galaxies, and the stars are referred to often in vast spatial compositions of floating lines and forms. His wife's paternal grandfather had been an astronomer. Her consequent interest in the subject, along with their physical proximity to the Griffith Observatory when they lived in the Los Angeles area, undoubtedly sparked Bertoia's cosmic reveries of the late forties and fifties.[22] Scientists he encountered at Point Loma reinforced these interests and broadened his knowledge and thinking.

All the sciences fascinated him—especially geology, physics, and archaeology, besides astronomy. Instead of novels, he read technical books, trying always to understand the nature of things. When he left California he gave his friend Oskar Fischinger two books he treasured, saying he might ask some day to have them back. They were *Wonders of Living Things* and *Wonders of Science Simplified*, published in 1943 and 1945 by Metro Publications, New York City. He was interested in the movement of the earth's tectonic plates as well as in atomic particles. The flight of a flock of birds intrigued him, why they all turn simultaneously. "I am always on the borderline of trying to be a scientist," he maintained in 1978.[23] (He had declared his interest in science much earlier on his application for entrance to Cranbrook in 1937.)

His wife Brigitta's interest in mysticism undoubtedly had considerable influence on Bertoia also. It was she who introduced her husband to the philosophy of Lao-Tzu through an English translation of the *Tao Te Ching*, or *Way of Life*. The simplicity advocated by the Tao as

well as its dualities of yang and yin, bright and dark, positive and negative, were profoundly appealing. He was further spurred in this direction by contact in California with the work of Mark Tobey and Morris Graves, both of whom he admired. In his life he embodied the humble, quiet, nonassertive nature of the Taoist, living simply and independently, close to nature, content with few material comforts, and devoted to his art. From early on, his work was affected by his reading about, and interpretation of, the Tao. He took to heart the admonition, "You shall give life to things but never possess them."[24] This—not modesty or lack of confidence—was the reason that he never wanted to sign his sculptures or graphics. He had no desire for possession, merely for creation. Nevertheless, he did seek acknowledgment of his efforts and accomplishments, as the controversy over the "Eames" chair and his patenting of *Sonambient* confirm.

Among other books of interest to Bertoia were D'Arcy Thomson's *Growth and Form*, St. John Perse's *Seamarks*, and a translation of Lucretius's *De rerum natura*.[25] In art books his tastes ran to the predictable ones on Klee, Rousseau, the Bauhaus, but he was also interested in Michelangelo and Leonardo, especially their writings. His bookshelves contained works on prehistoric cave drawings as well as modern painting, on the frescoes of Giotto as well as the woodcuts of Maillol and the letters of Van Gogh. He always read *Arts and Architecture, Scientific American,* and *Time,* and in later years he maintained subscriptions to a rather extensive list of periodicals that included *Smithsonian, Christian Science Monitor, National Geographic, Astronomy,* and *American Heritage,* among others. The list reveals the broad range of his intellect.

The contemporary artists whom Bertoia admired included, in addition to Tobey and Graves, Josef Albers, László Moholy-Nagy, and the sculptors, brothers Naum Gabo and Antoine Pevsner. Constructivism and the so-called realist sculpture of Gabo and Pevsner that followed it had introduced open form, assembling rather than modeling or carving, and the use of modern materials, ideas that promoted the kind of experimentation that pleased Bertoia. His familiarity with the work of Graves and Tobey no doubt resulted from his West Coast experience. Given his own already demonstrated leanings, the poetic fantasy of the former and the nonobjectivity of the latter were bound to appeal. He had frequent contact in the 1950s with Anni and Josef Albers, as the latter wished him to conduct a sculpture seminar at Yale.

Bertoia's interest in the works of Gabo and Pevsner brings to mind again the influence Bertoia's own sculpture had on his graphics. As indicated earlier in this chapter, he enjoyed working in both media, and consequently, the influences passed back and forth between them. In fact, it is often hard to say in which direction they proceeded. Certainly, drawing was his first artistic pursuit as a boy. His boyhood reminiscences of gypsies working on shiny copper pans were probably the source of his early bright, often golden, colors in both prints and sculpture. The precision of his metal craftsmanship, a technique he learned early at Cass Technical High School in Detroit, may have led to the precise geometry of the forms that made up his earliest graphic repertory. Later, the precisely machined materials—rods and wires—with which he worked on both chairs and sculpture seem recreated in the linear aspects of some of the monographics of the 1950s.

On the other hand, the brazing technique that Bertoia adopted in many of his sculptures may have been inspired by the interest in texture already evident in his graphic works. Similarly, the spill-casting technique pioneered by Bertoia in the 1960s, which resulted in spectacular textural effects produced by a remarkably painterly sculpture method, was undoubtedly brought on by the desire for a freer, more direct way of working with metal, one that, like his graphic technique, would allow the possibility of developing the accidental. In his graphics Bertoia had always sought the unexpected, the inner vision taking over, and adapted it to achieve his best results. Those results, occurring over a lifetime, may not be summed up in a single word.

The Results

First of all, there is the sheer volume of the work, some idea of which may be obtained from the graphics seen here. It should be borne in mind, however, that a selection like this can only *represent* what is judged to be Bertoia's best work; it cannot begin to encompass its totality. All the works shown here are from the collection that was left to Brigitta Bertoia in 1978. They are meant to be indicative of the nature and quality of the best that was produced in each of the four decades from the 1940s through the 1970s. As noted earlier, however, other examples do exist in museums as well as in the hands of private collectors.

From their beginnings at Cranbrook in 1940, the images were nonobjective. Using language based on aesthetic principles known to all artists, Bertoia composed with line, form, texture, and color. Those principles include a recognition of the stability of vertical and horizontal lines and shapes, the resurgence of the former and the repose of the latter; the dynamism of the diagonal and rhythmic repetition promoting a sense of motion; the timeless rigidity or rectilinearity and the freedom and restlessness of a curved line or shape; warm colors that project and cool ones that recede; complementaries that vibrate, producing tension. These and many more simple elements were used, for the most part intuitively, by Bertoia to create a response in the viewer and to stimulate thought. Only rarely did he begin with a desire to make a statement. It was usually the urge to paint or draw—the urge to create, not to imitate—that motivated the artist. But whether or not it was intended, the end product frequently does convey meaning, a meaning that has been arrived at often without his willing it and sometimes without his realizing it until the work was completed.

As a student of drawing and painting, Bertoia had been bored by the life classes. "There would be a model in front of us to draw. I would put down a line, a smudge. Impossible! How much better it seemed to let the line be a line and the smudge a smudge!"[26] Lines and smudges became his vocabulary, one through which he conveyed notions of poetic fantasy involving gentleness, mystery, firmness, excitement, turbulence—a full range of expression. Small, rapid, slashing strokes promote a feeling of frenzied activity, while broad sweeping lines from one end of the paper to the other denote an arm movement whose considerable force cannot help being translated to the viewer. Without imitating the natural world, he communicates its moods and meanings through his choices of stroke, color, and texture.

In Bertoia's earliest monographics, the stability of his squares and rectangles is enlivened by slanting lines and triangles. A soft, vaporous, smokey haze of background ink is counterbalanced by firmly drawn lines and shapes, the contrast deepening their mystery. A strong contour, often shadowed by a white line, is thus given emphasis and heightened meaning. Rhythmically repeated white lines drawn out of a dark background and superimposed on one another make cages of space that appear to float in and out of perspective vision. They have a nonrepresentational airiness and buoyancy like that of a Gaston Lachaise figure, producing similar sensations of lightness, gaiety, and elegance.

In examining this representative sampling, what strikes one immediately is the variety of motif. Whether predominantly linear or formal or combined linear and formal, the images presented in each decade are often widely dissimilar one to another. Within the nonrepresentational idiom, they are indicative of the varied interests of the artist as well as of his inventive capability. From precisely repeated geometries to the maelstrom of irregular smudges and wipes that characterize his more spontaneous works, there is no dearth of idea or monotony of image. At the same time, there is a progressive continuity in the variations on a single theme. The repeated geometric motif, for instance, moves from the hand-stamped woodblock prints of the early forties through several intermediary stages in which different printing techniques are adopted, to the prints of the fifties, which are closely allied to the metal sculpture screens produced at the same time. Linear images alternate throughout the decades between precise geometry and lyrical abandon. Abstractions based on nature influences gradually appear, at first in the form of cosmic references and then in what we may interpret as landscapes, cityscapes, tree and flower forms, and even the quasi-human figure. Interpretation is a personal matter. Each viewer brings to the image his or her own background of associations and derives from it a meaning often difficult to put into words but nevertheless real for that person. Bertoia believed the imagination (ours as well as his) to be infinitely more intriguing than the actual. Therefore, he made suggestions rather than statements in his images.

Cognate prints are a factor in sometimes as many as four versions of one idea. Bertoia's extensive use of the cognate, or afterimage, is one of the unique characteristics of his monographics. While many modern monotypists produce a second, paler print with variations, the usual practice of printing monotypes in a press limits the possibility of producing more than one such cognate. Bertoia's technique of brayer printing and/or hand rubbing allowed the ghostly reminiscence to remain and reregister often even after a reinking of the plate. This practice provided him with many of the accidental effects he then incorporated into successive prints. The resultant negatives harmonize with the vaporous textures of the printed inks, enhancing the effects of delicacy and softness. And yet each new print somehow avoids any sensation of monotony or appearance of muddiness. On the contrary, the presence of the ghostly images more often than not adds to the print an evanescent quality that improves it. Further, the use of cognates permitted Bertoia considerable opportunity to explore one of his favorite concepts, that of the negative and positive aspects of a single motif, a single form, a single curved line. He dealt with this concept in sculpture, too, but the reversal of dark and light in the graphics is more directly effective.

Rhythmic repetition, whether of line or of form, is a constant in Bertoia's work. It is seen in his curvilinear prints of the seventies as well as in his earliest, most precise rectilinear motifs. Most of the time it is carefully controlled. However, kinesis occasionally is seen to take over, especially in the larger graphics, where a sweeping arm movement communicates its energy by means of the stroke it produces.

The size of many of the prints is unusual, especially those from the fifties and sixties, when the plate used was often as large as twenty-four by thirty-nine inches. Because of the necessity for speed of execution to stay ahead of the drying inks, it is far more usual for monographics to be produced in much smaller format.[27] Although the early works varied considerably in size, some being as small as five by seven inches while others measured as much as forty-one by thirty inches, Bertoia's inclination was to work expansively. Characteristic, therefore, are the sweeping kinetics of many of his later drawings as the larger size gradually became the norm.

Rhythm and kinetics are aspects of Bertoia's lifelong concern with motion, seen early in his jewelry and consciously sought in his larger metal works. The teetering balance of his slender sculptures of 1947 culminated in the sounding pieces of the sixties and seventies. In the graphics, whether linear or formal, stabilized or floating, repetition conveys a sense of rhythm and therefore of movement. When the repetition is associated with a sense of arm or hand kinesis, the feeling achieved is of motion speeded up or intensified by emotion. Thus a new dimension is added. Many of the prints, especially from the fifties on, exhibit this intensification.

The keen sense of balance that governed the placing of a single tall form on a slender stem in the early sculptures, as well as the dimensions and placement of later works in their surroundings, can also be seen in Bertoia's graphics. Lines and forms float or stand in careful relationship both to each other and to the totality of the format. The chosen overall dimension appears to govern the placement of each inked mark. While many of the prints show evidence of the adaptation of accidental effects, they also exhibit a satisfying equilibrium born of Bertoia's innate sense of balance and proportion.

The ''happy accident,'' of course, was always eagerly anticipated and welcomed when it coalesced. Each surprise that revealed itself with the pulling of a print led to a new idea and another new work. It was one of the true delights of printmaking for Bertoia who, from the beginning, decried the monotony of print editions and set himself on the more interesting path of producing unique images. It was through the stimulation of the unexpected that he managed to achieve variety in his graphics even though, paradoxically, they were often composed of repetitive elements.

A concern for texture is apparent from beginning to end in Bertoia's prints. The monographics of the forties printed through repetitive hand stamping of a small block of wood are as tactile as the most unctuous oil painting. The soft, granular ink effect achieved through hand pressure from the back of the paper was a favorite throughout the decades, whether used as a ground line, for spatial effects, or to suggest modeling. It is often contrasted with hard, sharp line or the ghostly negatives of a cognate. Differentiations are made between soft and hard edges, thick and thin lines. Multiple striations are introduced, as well as sharp flecks and vaporous mists to vary the quality of surface characteristics and give illusionistic effects.

Textural variety was both the cause and the direct result of Bertoia's use of experimental tools and techniques. Since its introduction in the seventeenth century, the making of monotypes has been a process that lent itself to experimentation. The two basic methods—the additive, or light-field, and the subtractive, or dark-field—have both seen many different drawn or painted strokes produced through the use of a variety of implements—brushes, brush handles, sticks, rags, and fingers. The results have been as varied as the approaches. With the introduction of many new materials and gadgets in the twentieth century, artists have had a wider range of things from which to choose in making their marks, and the speed of execution often necessitates grabbing anything that happens to be at hand to use as an instrument. Bertoia enjoyed this aspect of the making of monographics. He deliberately chose or hastily adapted all manner of objects in order to produce a particular texture or density or sometimes just to see what effect they would have. Not only his fingers and thumbs, but the heel and back of his hand and even, once, his feet were used as implements.

His anticipatory excitement at the pulling of each print led Bertoia to eventually adopt exclusively the unusual technique of inking a plate, laying a blank sheet of paper over it, and drawing on the back of the paper with instruments that made no mark on it. As the work progressed he could see only dimly through the translucent paper what had already been drawn. Intuition took over (the "inner vision") and the mystery deepened until the final surprise of the pulled print. Additions to the surface or the use of a second plate took advantage of accidental or consciously achieved effects, often of great complexity. The techniques are so complex, in fact, as to cause great difficulty in their unraveling. In the sixties, as the pressure of time increased, simplicity became the order of the day, but the basic technique of drawing from the back of the paper prevailed. And in the seventies, again, Bertoia experimented with many new implements and techniques, including collage. In Una Johnson's words, "It has been the American artist's will to explore and his ability to accept and utilize change in a volatile environment that have given diversity, vigor, and a sense of exuberance to the many distinguished prints of this century."[28]

As a result of his joyous nature, Bertoia's monographics tend to elevate the spirit as well as delight the eye. Even in the time-pressed sixties when practical sculpture-related drawings prevailed, the images produced are often gently amusing. Shapes are irregular, lumpy, off-center, or slightly askew; lines meander playfully or form star- or flower-like structures or fantastic creatures. There is as lighthearted a feeling in the "frogs" and knotted filaments of the seventies as in the delicate linear geometries and bright golden colors of the forties. Permeating Bertoia's work is a sense of the blitheness of spirit governing the fanciful images. He once expressed it thus: "If I had to sum up my forty years as an artist I'd say my intent has always been the enrichment of life. I've avoided that which would depress man's mood or being. There's plenty in the newspapers of that. I want to show what's positive and joyful in the world. I like to see the beauty of a flower before I admit it will vanish in three days."[29]

To create delightful fantasies requires a delicate touch. This is seen in the fineness of line and softness of texture of Bertoia's monographics. Paradoxically, they often convey an impression of strength along with the delicacy. This is partly a result of the sureness of his strokes whether of firm outline or precise multiple repetition. It is as though each freehand line, form, or smudge is in exactly the right place, the place where the artist had intended from the beginning for it to be. As with oriental ink painting, there are no overdrawings, no corrected mistakes, hardly a mark that does not appear to have been intended. In some cases the strength of hand pressure is apparent where forms or shading are particularly emphasized and there is a seemingly inherent power in the image, so confident are the strokes that produced it.

Dichotomies proliferate in the work of Harry Bertoia: power and delicacy, strength and gentleness, certainty (sureness) and experiment, variety and yet considerable repetition, positive and negative, hard edge and soft, precision and randomness, control and the accidental are all encompassed in his oeuvre. It is a paradox that they exist in harmony side by side but perhaps no greater a paradox than the nature of the man himself.

Physically, he was stocky and powerfully built, capable of feats of strength. Yet he was soft-spoken, slow to anger, and gentle in his actions. He was both proud of his accomplishments and humble in his awareness of their place in the overall achievements of mankind. He had a logical, practical mind that figured accurate cost estimates and projected even for large sculpture works delivery dates his patrons could rely on. Yet the vision that guided him was an inner one fueled by dreams of poetic fantasy, lending a spirituality to his being and especially to his monographics, which were his most personal endeavor. Friends were particularly cognizant of his strength of character. In a handwritten letter that appears to acknowledge Bertoia's formal separation from Knoll in 1953, Hans Knoll wrote, "More than the need for your guidance in professional and esthetic matters I would like to feel free to continue to talk with you about some of the problems which like spider-webs surround our lives."[30]

One of the most revealing statements Bertoia ever made was written originally in February 1976 and reused as the opening statement in his posthumously printed *Fifty Drawings*. It is quoted here in full as a fitting conclusion to this survey of the most cherished phase of his life's work:

I did not start with a written credo or manifesto. Nor was there a program to be followed. It all came about very slowly. School days exposed me to the hows more than to the whys or the whats.

Encounters with the work of others were stimulants to broader vistas. Childhood memories, mostly happy ones, persisted. Nature as an influence, always strong.

Companionship, love and family, a measure of fulfillment. Social contact and hours of solitude, all ingredients in the process of one's growth.

Enthusiastic beginnings and recognition of failures marking a long quest to seek and sometimes find a form, a structure, a sound or a way. A find that would tend to make me feel what I am or one that would cause a change in me, would simply deepen the mystery. Facing a problem, yes. Solving it, more often than not, would prove evanescent.

The acceptance of the reality of the dream as a stimulant and propellant toward achieving the other reality generated an atmosphere of involvement rather than passivity. Immersion into the vast recesses of the mind leading to the realization that this inner world is as immense as the cosmos outside. . . .

At this eternal moment, I have a gut feeling that awareness of the miracle of life is the purpose of life. I might never know."[31]

5. The Catalog

Text for the color plates that immediately follow this page will be found in the black-and-white section of the catalog under the corresponding plate number.

All works are untitled, undated, and unsigned. Where possible, a date (year) has been assigned. Otherwise, the monographics are grouped according to decade.

Dimensions are given in inches for both image and paper, height first.

All works are from the collection of Brigitta Bertoia except as noted. Plates 1, 48, 54, and 55 were sold between the time of initiation and publication of this book.

Plate 1.

Plate 3.

Plate 5.

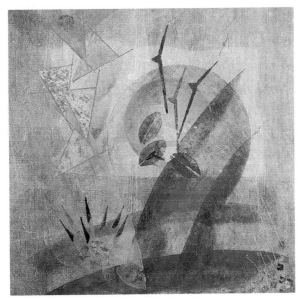

Plate 6.

Plate 8.

Plate 12.

Plate 15.

Plate 20.

Plate 21.

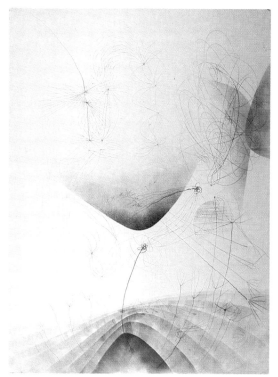

Plate 22.

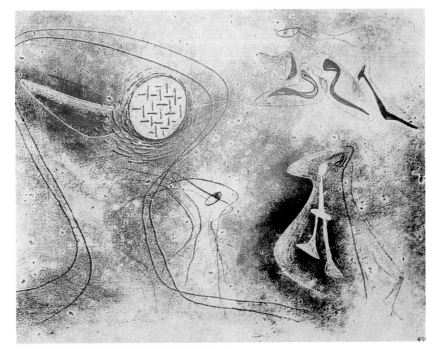

Plate 23.

Plate 31.

Plate 41.

Plate 47.

Plate 61.

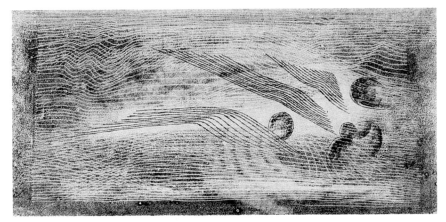

Plate 72.

The 1940s

Bertoia's monotypes and other monographics of the forties established the precedent for his work in this medium for the next forty years. There were basically two methods of producing the images, one based on form and the other on line, and he used different techniques for each. The techniques were of basic importance to the results produced.

The precision of geometry is an early fascination first seen in prints made from repetitively stamped and highly textured forms and somewhat later adapted to more irregular, imaginative, even capricious approaches (plates 4, 5, and 6). Imagination of another kind takes over in the works of fantasy involving wandering lines used sometimes almost geometrically (plate 12), sometimes quite randomly (plates 15 and 22), as well as in those concerned with form (plates 8 and 25).

Fantasy and geometry are the two major components of Bertoia's imagery during the forties, and both were eventually translated from graphics into metal sculpture. The former is seen in the precariously balanced rod-and-wire constructions and the so-called landscape fantasies of the late forties and early fifties which, according to one reviewer are "based on a slab of sandstone or ebony or metal in which holes have been bored to hold vertical steel wires balancing on their ends bell shapes. . . . He does not imitate nature as Calder does; he is in competition with nature and wants to make it over again."[1] The more geometric graphics are responsible for the basic structure and texture of the sculpture screens of the fifties, which marked Bertoia's first successful collaborations with architects.

Within both basic types of imagery, there is a fascination with negative and positive ambiguities. Both dark against light, and light against dark, lines and forms are seen in many of the prints, but plates 8 and 14 are most revealing of this interest. The use of linear shadowing, in which a white or negative line "ghosts" the positive by following it closely can be seen to advantage in plate 13 especially, though it appears elsewhere as well. Effects of transparency and other sorts of spatial ambiguity, perhaps an influence from cubism, are also seen in numerous works both geometric and fantastic.

Except for plate 25 and perhaps plate 6, all monographics of the forties shown here present their images as floating in space, and more often than not the space in which they float is indicated by the granular texture of the ink lying on the surface of the paper. The soft, vaporous quality of this background ink texture pleased Bertoia very much, and he continued to adopt the printing technique that produced it. The dry, crusty texture of the repetitive geometrics (especially as seen in plates 1, 2, and 3) has a much more tactile quality, a quality that, translated to metals through the process known as brazing, characterized the sculptures of the fifties and part of the sixties.

Bertoia's color preferences in the first decade tended toward the warm hues—reds, oranges, yellows—often used in high intensities and occasionally in the company of their complementaries. This is especially true in the more precise geometric works (plates 1 and 3) but the bright colors were also used in more sparing touches in works of fantasy (plates 8, 10, and 23). Generally speaking, however, these were printed in more subdued tones and tints of the primaries as well as of red-brown, blue-gray, and black. Few monochromatic works were produced during the forties, although a trend may have been developing in that direction toward the end of the decade.

Many variations exist in the type, size, and shape of the paper used by Bertoia during the forties. Among those published here, the smallest image measures less than five by seven inches on very thin tissue paper (plate 15) while the largest is printed on illustration board 41⅛-inches high by 30⅜-inches wide (plate 22), and there is a multitude of sizes in between. There are few clearly intended horizontal formats, even fewer definite verticals; most could be either horizontal or vertical compositions.

Many of the early works, especially the heavily textured geometrics but also some of the others, are printed on heavy paper like map paper or illustration board. Later in the decade, the printing is done more and more frequently on rice paper until that becomes standard and a finer type of laid rice paper makes its appearance.

Plate 1 (early 1940s)

Colored inks and oils on heavy paper
Image: 20¾ × 32½; paper: 21⅛ × 32¾
Private Collection, Pottstown, Pennsylvania

This and the next two monographics can be securely dated to the early 1940s. They are characterized by their precise geometric forms and their use of brilliant colors, strong textural effects, heavy paper, and generally large size. The fact that their compositions can be considered from either a vertical or a horizontal standpoint is also characteristic. The sculpture screens produced by Bertoia in the 1950s for General Motors, Manufacturers Hanover Trust, and the Massachusetts Institute of Technology Chapel are closely related to these graphics.[2]

In the present plate, a module was chosen, a near square, measuring 2¼ by 2⅛ inches. A block of such dimensions was cut out of wood and used to pick up ink and stamp it on the surface of a very heavy paper on which dark blue shading to blue-green ink had first been rolled and dried. The block was successively coated with one or more brightly colored inks and hand stamped repeatedly, side by side, in regular rows covering or almost covering the ground. Sometimes the blue-green shows through at the edges of squares, between rows, or where the other inks did not adhere or completely cover. Unevenness of pressure and deliberate overlapping of some of the "squares," as well as the use of bright, warm colors on top of less intense, cool colors help to produce an effect of more than one plane in depth. Here and there a "square" was outlined in white or black ink, reinforcing this effect. The result is a highly colorful, textured surface of precise forms that seem to exist three-dimensionally in several planes. (See also color plate.)

Plate 2 (early 1940s)

Colored inks and oils on heavy paper
Image: 19¾ × 28; *paper:* 20¼ × 28¼

The technique here is the same as in plate 1 except that it
is more complex. A rectangular form was stamped over
an uneven light-to-medium-blue background in colors
ranging from dark blue to yellow-green, yellow, orange,
and red. The module is 6¼-inches long and 1¼-inches
wide at its narrowest end, spreading slightly to 1½-inches
wide. The overlapping of the forms produced considerable intermixing of the colors and created rectilinear
shapes of other, smaller dimensions than those of the
module. In many areas, the blue of the undercoat was allowed to show through so that this color predominates.
Several linear definitions were added, and a second module in the form of a short, narrow bar was stamped in a
variety of colors in just a few places on top of the other
forms. The effect of this print is one of transparency and
pronounced planar depths, as though rectangular pieces
of colored glass were stretched on cords, one behind another, in front of an open window. In fact, as early as
1943, Bertoia's first three-dimensional experiment using a
module was constructed in a similar fashion, and in 1967
he realized a completed sculpture commission as a window screen.[3]

Plate 3 (early 1940s)

Colored inks and oils on heavy buff paper watermarked
"Unbleached Arnold"
Image: 24½ × 37⅝; paper: 24⅞ × 38

Repeated trapezoids were printed in the same manner as
in plate 1—the rows regular and the units densely packed
and only occasionally overlapping on a dark green, black,
and blue-green ground. Edges of the forms are sometimes
hard, sometimes soft, depending on pressure and color
intensity. The trapezoids were placed with the wide end
alternately at the top and bottom, achieving greater density. The colors of the trapezoids range from bright red to
yellow, from pink to pastel blue-green. The dark background is allowed to show through in only a very few
places. Superimposed over the trapezoids are lines of
varying delicacy in black, red, yellow, and light blue-
green ink. Each group of lines is in a single color, and
they radiate, for the most part, from a single point forming a more or less triangular surface pattern that ties together a composition that can be read effectively from
any of its four sides. (See also color plate.)

Plate 4 (1940s)

Colored inks on tissue rice paper
Image: 6⁷⁄₁₆ × 9; paper: 6⅝ × 9¼

This is one of a further group of works using precise geometric form in a varied and irregular manner. They are
printed on thin paper like rice paper or tissue and are generally small and intimate in size, and their colors are less
brilliant, often soft and granular. Their geometric forms
remain hard-edged and precise but there is more variety
in each work and the forms are frequently randomly scattered rather than rigidly repeated in rows. The technique
of stamping with cutout modules is used in these works
also, but with variations, and often combined with other
printing methods.

Plate 4 is a truly tiny one done on very thin tissue-like
paper with a hard surface. The background is a soft, granular, medium brown shading almost to white at center.
Strokes of the brayer used to apply the background ink
are visible around the edges. The geometric units are trapezoids of at least five different sizes and shapes and have
been stamped on the surface of the print, often overlapping each other. The colors vary in intensity, the large
nearly central red trapezoid being the brightest. Red
forms predominate but are balanced by their varying tints
and tones as well as by the variety of greens and yellow-
greens among the other forms, a composition of complementaries.

Plate 5 (1940–43)

Colored inks on thin paper
Image: 16¼ × 13; *paper:* 20¾ × 15⅜

Triangles of many different shapes and sizes compose
plate 5, which has been matted vertically. Ranged in rows
on top of a golden yellow ground along the bottom edge
are large isosceles triangles shaded from dark to light
gray and pierced at their bases by smaller, lighter triangles. At the left margin are smaller ones in shades of
gray-green. Short isosceles triangles and narrow, angled
lancets in tones of brown shading to gold line up along
the top and upper right side. Most of these have a more
or less transparent appearance, whereas superimposed on
top of them in a more random fashion are small paired
triangles of greater opacity—brown with golden yellow,
black with orange, brown and blue-green, blue-green and
orange. Some of the latter are of high intensity but the
general overall effect is soft and shadowy due to the granular texture of most of the larger forms. It was works
such as this, done on translucent paper, which were
sometimes framed between two sheets of glass for display with a light source behind, thus enhancing effects of
transparency and three-dimensionality. (See also color
plate.)

Plate 6 (1942)

Colored inks on rice paper
Image: 10 × 10; *paper:* 13⅜ × 12

In a square format, plate 6 presents both curvilinear and rectilinear forms on a soft gray ground that is lighter at center than around the edges. A large gray circle slightly off-center is overprinted with a smaller one in yellow-green shading to yellow. Two gray arcs made by a brayer angle cross the circles toward the right on top of two other arcs that swing across the bottom of the page horizontally, their hard, convex edges upward, their inner edges vaporized, disappearing into nothingness. Crossing the face of the smaller circle and overlapping the larger are several forms colorfully stamped in triplicate—trapezoids, paired lunettes, and long and short tapered bars joined to each other at a slight angle by triangular projections. Tumbling down the left side of the page and scattered elsewhere throughout are small triangles and circles in mottled green, yellow-green, yellow, and orange with red-orange accents. In the lower right corner tiny trapezoids are sprinkled in gray, black, and light-blue with light-blue angled lines emanating upward and toward center.

Using a multitude of geometric forms in a square format, this composition is oriented toward a particular view, seeming in some areas to suggest ground lines and growth patterns. It reads well only in the position shown. Only a color photograph can reveal its subtleties. Its small size and subdued color as well as the informal, arbitrary placement of its elements give it an intimacy and sense of mystery not shared by the larger, more precise geometric works. This monographic has been dated 1942 by Brigitta Bertoia, who believes its origin to have been in oriental philosophy. (See also color plate.)

Plate 7 (1940s)

Colored inks on rice paper
Image: 17⅞ × 24⅞; *paper:* same dimensions

Unlike the previous monographics, which are geometry-oriented, the next four contain fantastic images. The forms are given humanoid characteristics, but by no stretch of the imagination could they be construed to represent human beings. Ghostly white lines or forms often reveal the presence of a cognate print.

Here, a figure rises out of nothingness at the lower left corner. It is described by a more or less continuous white line that sweeps around two wide-flung areas separated by a very narrow joining and continues after a long, narrow "neck" to circumscribe a modified triangular terminal area at upper right. Both inside and outside the figure many lines, both negative and positive, repetitively follow the contours or describe vortices (one of the latter covers the upper-left quarter of the print). The triangular terminus of the figure is given the suggestion of a head by the use of shading, two round white areas for eyes, and an open, *V*-shaped mouth from which emanates what appears to be a soft vapor. The portion of the figure just below the long neck is given the appearance of a torso by its winglike shape and two symmetrically placed vortices. The deep red-brown area of its base, however, with its open-ended beginning and the egg nucleus to the right (possibly the suggestion of a fetus) emphasize the genie-escaped-from-a-bottle effect of the whole as it floats in space. The mark seen in the photograph just below and to the right of the small circle is a tear in the paper.

The colors are subdued, merging almost imperceptibly into one another, and generalized rather than local—gray-blue across the top and at right, yellow from the left into the center, red-brown across the entire lower half, with gray-blue again at the bottom edge. Here the technique involved spreading the inks on a plate, drawing and wiping directly in the inks to produce white areas and lines, then additional drawing from the back of the paper plus brayer or hand pressure to pick up the image. Straight white lines may be detected from a previous print made on the same plate, but they have not been adapted to this drawing.

Plate 8 (1940s)

Colored inks on rice paper
Image: 17¾ × 23¾; *paper:* same dimensions

The overall background of this monographic is gray tend-
ing toward brown at the top. Its forms are complex, beginning with a number of overlapping and seemingly transparent monochromatic shapes somewhat in the cubist
manner at upper left. Unlike those of cubism, however,
the transparent planes generally have rounded corners
except where two sharp angles penetrate a small oval
area, which is colored bright red. A single, angled vertical
white line with a dot at its upper end traverses the gray
area connecting it to a large oval shape, narrowed at both
ends, in the bottom-left corner.

Rising through the middle of the print is a ghostly figure reminiscent of the one in plate 7 while at right is outlined a huge shape in the form of an inverted curved-
angle triangle whose descending point is truncated by a
darker gray horizontal oval, open-ended at the right edge
of the paper. Within this oval the sides of the upper triangle appear to continue, curving at first toward each other
and then away. Below the oval a continuous white line
defines two large descending loops of irregular shape
separated by a light gray area in which are described
many soft, swirling lines, both light and dark. The right
descending loop is filled with small geometric figures colored yellow, black, and dark red, picking up the spotty
touches of color used elsewhere in the print.

The technique here involves the use of a cognate,
which provides most of the negative material on the left,
as well as both painting on the plate and scratching into
the wet painted ink, as seen in the right half. There has
also been some drawing on the back of the paper and
possibly also directly on the surface. The complexity of
the technique matches the complexity of the composition,
which is intriguing in its combination of geometric with
humanoid forms. (See also color plate.)

Plate 9 (1940s)

Colored inks on rice paper
Image: 17⅞ × 23⅞; *paper:* 18 × 24

Plate 10 (1940s)

Colored inks on rice paper
Image: 17 × 23¾; *paper:* same dimensions

These two monographics exemplify the use of a cognate
to produce a variant on a theme. Plate 9 was done first,

in part by scratching and wiping into the wet red brown
inks rolled onto the glass plate in three vertical areas. In
plate 10 yellow, green, and dark blue inks were added
elsewhere, giving the cognate a considerably more colorful appearance than its predecessor.

In the original, three fantastic forms emerge from dark
holes in a flat cloudlike shape and rise to float on a mottled background filled with lazily curving linear vapor
trails. The central form, resembling in its general shape
the genie figures of plates 7 and 8, vanishes at the top
edge in the cognate because the paper there is seven-

eighths of an inch shorter. The other two forms rise on stems to broadly spreading, flat oval tops like mushrooms growing one on top of another.

Contrasts are strong in plate 9, and the lines, whether negative or positive, are distinct. In plate 10 the lines and forms are less vigorous in appearance, creating a softer effect in keeping with the ghostly aspects of the image reversals there. Areas left white or almost white in the earlier print have picked up the residue of ink to become dark in plate 10 while dark areas have become light. Some additional strokes were made from the back of the

cognate, and many fine lines were added in black ink on the surface of the pulled print. These are especially noticeable on the right side, across the bottom, and in the rising figure at left. See also the discussion of plates 9 and 10 in the chapter on techniques, page 35.

Plate 11 (1945–47)

Colored inks and oils on heavy map paper
Image: 24 × 36; *paper:* 26 × 37⅝

The characteristic use of line seen here has its corollary in
the repetitively stamped geometric forms of the same period, though the technique is quite different. Here, first
blue, then black, ink was rolled directly on the heavy
white paper. Overlapping triangles, circles, and trapezoids were then inscribed with a stylus into the still wet
ink down to the surface of the paper in some cases. Delicate geometric figures were produced freehand by first
describing the outer limits, then repeating the line many
times in ever smaller configurations within the original
enclosure until the center was reached. Or, a line began
at a single point and continued uninterruptedly, freely cir-
cumscribing itself until its outer limit defined a geometric
figure. As Bertoia put it in a statement about drawing published in 1944, the line "spends its energy and comes to
an equilibrium equivalent to a life-cycle."[4] Linear tracings
in colored inks overlap those inscribed into the surface.

   This monographic is dated between 1945 and 1947 because a tag from the Nierendorf Gallery is fixed to the
back.

Plate 12 (1940s)

Colored inks, metallic ink, and powdered metal on rice paper
Image: 22 × 30⅞; *paper:* same dimensions

Both this and plate 11, which resembles it in technique, are quite large in size, plate 11 measuring exactly two feet by three feet and the present work being only slightly smaller. They were probably done in California, but smaller works like them are to be seen in the Cranbrook collection as well. In some, linear spirals, swirls, and comet tails streak across the page with great abandon reminding us of fireworks or of shooting stars in the sky on a jet-black August night or, more prosaically, of a sheet of inspired doodles produced intuitively during attendance at a dull meeting. The linear figures which seem to have accidentally disported themselves around the rectangular spaces produce compositions of exquisite occult balance and satisfying unity.

The background ink here has a more granular appearance than in the previous plate, and some of the white linear figures may represent the residue of a cognate. Gold metallic dust was used over large portions of the work prior to the application of any of the superimposed lines, perhaps to aid drying of the background as well as to create a shimmering effect. Drawn on the surface were additional geometries in gold metallic and pink inks creating a three-dimensional web of shining, delicate filaments. (See also color plate.)

Plate 13 (1940s)

Colored inks on rice paper
Image: 17⅞ × 23¾; *paper:* same dimensions

In this and the next monographic, repetitive line is used in a nongeometric manner. In both works the negative or white lines form a network of interconnected parallels that turn rounded corners from vertical to horizontal and back again like the complex electrical circuitry Bertoia may have seen at Point Loma.[5] Positive lines tend to be straight and mostly vertical, with tiny circles or triangles at their beginnings and endings from which wiry filaments occasionally proceed in chaotic confusion. The delineations, both negative and positive, float on a vaporous background of imperceptibly merging brown, red-brown, gray, and orange-yellow ink. The positive lines, drawn from the back, take on the color of each ink as they pass through it. Some shadowing is seen—positive lines and dots are closely followed by negatives—as in the ghost of an image on a television screen. This adds liveliness and an effect of three-dimensionality to each thin line or round dot. Soft smudges of background ink accentuate the delicacy of the linear treatment.

Plate 14 (1940s)

Colored inks on rice paper
Image: 17¾ × 23¾; *paper:* same dimensions

The use of a template and a second plate has created a broad white rectangle situated just below center and slightly to the right, acting as a kind of magnifying window. As the positive vertical lines appear to pass through the rectangle, they become thicker and change to intense hues of black, brown, green, red, or yellow. The lines within the rectangle are accompanied by broad, vertical striations of the same brightly colored inks in a granular texture much coarser than that of the background. At left inside the "window" are many fine verticals that begin and end there, not passing through. Hovering behind the rectangle at center are the upper and lower arcs of circles. Above, just left of center, is a continuous, meandering contour with many indentations and protrusions both above and below a generally horizontal area. Gray shading in places both within the contour and outside the contour gives an effect of negative-positive ambiguity.

Shadowing and a whimsical play of negative and positive combine with precision and delicacy of line to create an intriguing composition. While the lines of plate 14 are more rigid than those of plate 13, all are displayed effectively against backgrounds of a variegated, but uniformly soft, texture, emphasizing the linear precision by contrast.

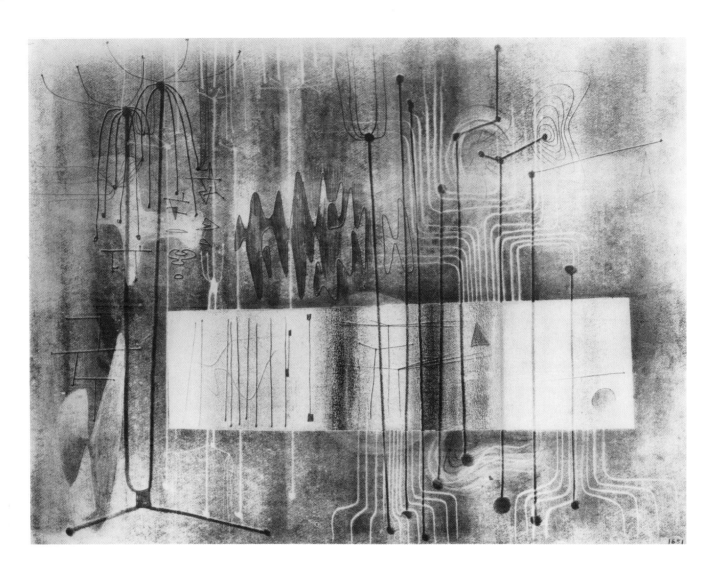

Plate 15 (1943)

Colored inks on rice paper
Image: 6⅞ × 5; paper: 7⅞ × 6⅝

Working with line in a freer, more random fashion, Bertoia produced another group of prints of considerable divergence in their size, the type of paper on which they are printed, and the nature of their visual images. The smallest is the present plate which is just under seven by five inches and is on rice paper.

This small work is the most colorful and has the most accidental appearance of the group. On a smooth background of blue-green and orange-pink appear thick and thin lines of deep orange, yellow, dark green, blue, and pale blue-green, some of which are more or less parallel, though some angle across the paper at different degrees. Most begin and end with either a point or a knot of curved lines or a starlike radiation of short lines. Other groups of more delicate lines curve in parallels to form airy ovoids of crisscrossing direction. This work strongly suggests a "stream of consciousness" played out against and floating in a fathomless, dreamlike space. Its size, colors, and paper type relate it to the "Graphic Poem" done for Mrs. Valentiner, and it is therefore datable to 1943. (See also color plate.)

Plate 16 (1940s)

Black and brown-black ink on heavy paper watermarked
"Van Gelder Zonen Holland"
Image: 24 × 36⅛; *paper:* 25 × 38¼

Some of the same linear ideas as those of plate 15 are
used here but with a much greater sense of order and virtually monochrome on heavy paper more than three feet
wide. Shadowed parallel verticals with dotted or scribbled beginnings and endings march across the page in a
semblance of symmetry, longest lines at the outside
edges, gradually diminishing in length and interval toward the center where the single shortest line appears to
be receding in space. Linear ovoids and a few horizontals
float lightly behind the ranged verticals, while above, a
series of irregular loops drawn in a centrifugal manner
create a flowerlike image. Radiating from the center of
this "flower" are broad, soft strokes made by finger pressure on the back of the paper. Like octopus tentacles or
ribbons blowing in the wind they undulate as they trail
off into the void. The vaporous effect of the background
ink, fairly strong at top and bottom edges of the plate but
shading to nothing at center, enhanced by the surface texture of the heavy paper, produces an illusion of cosmic or
oceanic vastness through which the linear structures lazily move. This slow movement is similar to that of the
flexible metal rods Bertoia used in the sixties and seventies for his sounding sculptures. He found a corollary to
that movement (after the fact) in the sea plants and ani-
mals he saw underwater in the Bahamas.[6]

Plate 17 (1940s)

Colored inks on rice paper(?)
Image: 18 × 23⅞; *paper:* same dimensions

Random, wandering aspects of line are explored more thoroughly in this most painterly of the linear prints. The entire page is covered with swirling lines, some soft and thick as a finger, others fine and delicate as hair; some in large, sweeping curves, others in intricate loops. Thick or thin, grand or minute, the freehand lines follow one another closely and repetitively. Many positive (inked) lines shadow negative (white) ones, which may have been wiped or scratched from the inked plate.

A number of different drawing tools were used for this print, from brushes to fingers and thumbs, from blunt-ended sticks or other instruments to extremely fine scratching and ink-carrying points. Red-brown, purple, and yellow inks were rolled on the plate in broad areas merging with each other and were picked up on the surface of the paper by the use of the various implements from the back as well as by brayer and hand rubbing. The effect is of a swirling maelstrom of broad and turbulent motion. The comparison that comes most readily to mind is with Leonardo's studies of the movement of water.

Plate 18 (1940s)

Black and red-brown ink on rice paper
Image: 17½ × 23¼; paper: 17⅞ × 24

Lines with beginnings and endings were a frequent motif
with Bertoia, and the present plate is yet another example
of the uses to which he put them. Here, both negative
and positive, short, curved lines, each with a dot at either
end, appear to float on the paper randomly crisscrossing
each other to form a surface pattern over the top of doz-
ens of tiny line drawings. Many of the latter reflect images used in other prints of the forties. These delicate linear doodles are scattered throughout and may have been
drawn either directly on the paper or on the plate which
was then inked lightly with black around the edges and
red-brown circling the center. The thick, negative, curved
lines were scratched into the wet ink while the granular
texture and the heavy, positive curves are the result of
hand and implement pressure from the back of the paper
after it was laid over the plate. The overall effect is not
unlike the ''white writing'' of Mark Tobey or a more controlled rendition of the linear dribbles of Jackson Pollock
and some of the other abstract expressionist painters of
the time.[7] Here there is a randomness, and yet a rhythm
that produces unity.

Plate 19 (late 1940s?)

Colored inks on laid rice paper
Image: 32 × 23; *paper:* 34 × 24

A compendium of line-drawn motifs similar to those in plate 18 is seen here, this time in considerably larger size and without the unifying surface pattern. Over seventy-five individual black ink drawings, many overlapping each other, appear in a work that could be considered from either a horizontal or vertical viewpoint (it seems obviously to have been worked on from at least three sides). Some of the by now familiar images include free-flowing repetitive lines, climbing mushroom shapes, vertical lines with dots at either end, repeated modules, and lines radiating from a central core.

The work is enlivened with spotty touches of granular textured color—orange, yellow, light and dark blue, as well as brown and gray. As in several of the previously discussed prints, the random nature of its scattered linear scribblings would give the impression of a simple doodle sheet were it not for the strong sense of compositional balance that pervades the whole. Seen from any of its four sides this monographic exhibits a surprising cohesiveness while at the same time impressing us with its diversity.

The structural nature of many of the individual drawings in this print is an indication that this work was done at a time when Bertoia was beginning to work three-dimensionally. Although it is believed to have been done in the late forties, the possibility cannot be ruled out that it may date from the early fifties. Certainly, many of the individual ideas represented eventually evolved into sculptures, some of them as late as in the sixties and seventies. In any case, it may well be the graphic work Bertoia referred to in 1955 as the "one I refer to as a 'map' and 'genesis' of my world of art. It is from this single graphic that I find an endless source of suggestions for growth and development. In its accidentals I find, as in Nature, sublime rationality, that brings forth what is truly enjoyable."[8]

Plate 20 (1940s)

Colored inks on rice paper(?)
Image: 18 × 12; *paper:* same dimensions

One of a group of works combining both line and form, this monographic displays a variety of both solid and linear geometric figures—circles, triangles, trapezoids, figure-eights, and simple intersecting straight and curved lines—in a format influenced by cubism in its angular division of the composition. The geometric figures tend to be linear and grouped when small, whereas the larger ones are widely scattered and generally represented as solid.

There is considerable evidence of wiping of the plate and a strong emphasis on the play of negative against positive, including the "ghosting" of the linear geometries of the lower-right corner. In some cases the white, or negative, lines seem to have been pulled out of the ink first. The positive lines shadowing the triangles, circles, figure-eights, and so on, of the group in the lower-right corner were drawn in black ink on the back of the paper, the only lines or forms thus visible.

The print is colorful in generalized areas—marked off by angular lines—of red-brown, blue, yellow, and black as well as in local touches such as the yellow and white triangle in a blue field that joins point to point with a dark red-brown and blue triangle in a lighter brown field. Delicate lines in both blue and brown ink have been added here and there to the surface of the print, most noticeably at lower left. (See also color plate.)

Plate 21 (1940s)

Colored inks on rice paper
Image: 17⅞ × 23⅞; *paper:* same dimensions

Apparently influenced by cubism, perhaps more directly
than plate 20, is this work, with its many small, angular
facets treated by shading in the cubist manner so as to
appear transparent and overlapping. Unlike cubism, however, there is no representational basis even though the
generally warm tonality, the radiant "suns" at left, and
the tiny "Joshua tree" figures tend to make one think of a
desert landscape. It is rather a composition of triangles,
trapezoids, and sectors that could as well be considered
to be floating on air or scintillating underwater were it
not for the disposition of the colors. These lie in horizontal bands of red-brown, yellow, and orange softly merging one into the other with gray-blue near the top and
repeated across the bottom. Many fine, mostly dark
brown lines were added to the surface of the print in all
color areas enhancing the cubist effect of transparent
planes. (See also color plate.)

Plate 22 (1944)

Colored inks on illustration board
Image: 41⅛ × 30⅜; *paper:* same dimensions

More numerous and more interesting than the works combining geometric forms and lines are those dealing in fantasy. Probably inspired by the works of Odilon Redon, Paul Klee, and surrealism, they often combine "taking a line for a walk" (Klee's phrase) with capricious or ominous forms.

This is the largest of all the monographics. It is done on illustration board about one-eighth of an inch thick, the edges and corners of which are beginning to crumble. The method of its printing remains a mystery. The series of curved "hill" forms rising from the lower edge and the ominously hovering "clouds," all in a brownish green color, could have been accomplished with the edge of a brayer applied directly to the paper board. In the "hills" the successive rollings without reinking produced a gradually weaker and weaker impression. This method, however, does not explain the more or less vertical streaks running through the brayer striations. More mysterious yet is the manner of transference of the many delicate lines scattered throughout in colors of red, orange, yellow, green, and blue. Some of them start out one color and wind up another, most notably the strong curved vertical at bottom center, which begins its life in a bright red scribble at the top and gradually, almost imperceptibly becomes dark green as it descends into the "hills." This and other similar lines could not have been drawn directly on the board. Yet, how were they transferred?[9]

Technique aside, the forms and lines combine to create a fantasy of cosmic dimensions. The hovering forms in their color and density matching those of the "hills" beneath make one think of Earth and its satellites, natural and man-made. Are these giant meteors or missiles about to descend and destroy an already barren Earth? Or are they remnants of a mushroom cloud that has already wreaked its destruction? The suggested threat of the large opposing forms is counteracted delightfully and optimistically by the delicacy, the color, and the playfulness of the lines. They convey different notions by their delicacy or firmness, their directness or random wandering, their beginnings and endings or lack of same. If this be Earth below, it floats through space along with the other planets of the solar system, lines of growth rising up from it. Many interpretations are, of course, possible in such a fantasy. (See also color plate.)

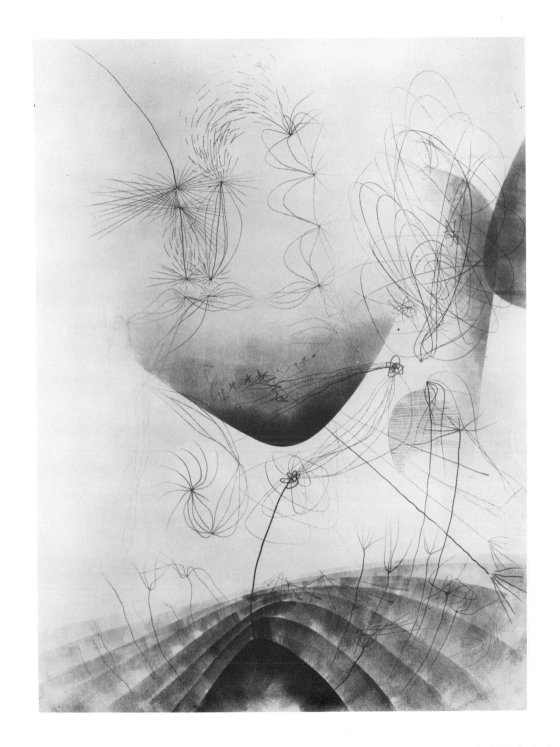

Plate 23 (1940s)

Colored inks on laid rice paper
Image: 6½ × 8⅝; *paper:* same dimensions

In contrast to the large size of plate 22, the present print
measures barely six by nine inches and contains some
rather spotty but vivid color areas. A large, flat-headed
linear loop runs through red, blue, and orange areas just
left of center, its ends turning inward toward the bottom
to form a constriction and then trailing off to right and
left. To the upper right, inside the loop, a circle is drawn
around an area of the paper left white. The circle contains
many short, unconnected vertical and horizontal lines
and is surrounded by short, curving lines in a manner
that seems to indicate directional turning. Streaming out
to the left, a line forming a winglike structure has been
scratched through red ink. A much shorter, fainter
"wing" is scratched through the orange area to the right
of the circle. Two variations of the loop motif are seen,
much smaller, at lower center and at right. Instead of a
circle the right-hand loop contains a humanoid shape
scratched out of the black and orange inks.

In the upper-right corner, blue and ochre lines have
been added to the surface of the print describing curvate
shapes, some birdlike and some serpentine, sometimes
one within the other. The loops appear to have a gravita-
tional orientation and combine with the humanoid and
faunal references to negate the otherwise astral aspects of
the design. Such whimsical touches as the winged, whirl-
ing "sun" and the birds with the worms inside remind
one of Picasso's fish in a bird cage and birds in a fishbowl
of his *Peace* mural at Vallauris, done in 1952. Plate 23 can
be fairly securely dated in the decade of the forties, however, because of its size and its vivid coloration. (See also
color plate.)

Plate 24 (1940s)

Colored inks on laid rice paper
Image: 12 × 16⅝; *paper:* same dimensions

The composition is divided into levels by more or less
horizontal lines, each of which is connected to the next
by three verticals. A hovering birdlike figure at top appears to gather in the three verticals of the topmost level
and the whole structure seems, therefore, to dangle hap-
hazardly from above in a rather precarious framework.
Within each level floats a different set of forms, most of
which can by now be recognized as belonging to the forties, like those already seen in plates 7, 8, 18, and 19. The
genie figure is seen in horizontal position in the second
level from the bottom and has been given added surrealist attributes of clearly defined holes in its several protu-
berances. The curvaceous shapes formed by repetitive
lines in the lowest level will be taken up again in the late
sixties and seventies in drawings and in small sculptures
made of welded copper rods. Colors here are somewhat
subdued—red-brown, brown, and black—except for a
touch of yellow in the middle level, and all lines and
forms are positive, drawn from the back of the paper laid
over the inked plate.

Plate 25 (late 1940s?)

Black and brown ink on laid rice paper
Image: 11¾ × 16⅜; *paper:* same dimensions

Bertoia's colors of the fifties become considerably more
subdued, and it is possible, therefore, that this monographic, done in brown and black ink on laid rice paper,
may be from the early years of that period. However, its
balancing verticals with their beginning and ending dots
relate closely to other graphics of the forties, particularly
plates 13 and 14, probably done sometime after 1945.
That, along with other considerations, makes it seem
more logically placed here.

A cognate has provided a number of white verticals as
well as several small unidentifiable curvaceous shapes.
Added are the tall, slender poles with balancing rods
across their tops provided with stabilizing bases (as were
the "Joshua trees" of plate 21). The forms are scattered
and appear to be standing, albeit on different levels. The
largest form is central and is drawn and shaded to look
like a mechanical monster facing, on its right, a totally
nonhuman shape made up of two tall, tapering curves
balanced on the apex of a triangular base. A smaller, humanoid form (bifurcated base topped by arms, neck, and
head with eyes) at left and a still smaller shape at far
right resembling nothing human or animal complete the
picture.

Here for the first time we are getting close to something that resembles, however distantly, a peopled landscape rather than lines and forms floating in space. The
forms stand rather than float although there is as yet no
horizon or ground line. Some of them even cast shadows.
They tempt us to concoct a story involving the monster
and the lady. But Bertoia stops well short of supplying
details. Our imagination is given free rein in this night-
marish scene of menacing figures and devices balanced
by soft ghostly creatures receding into the night.

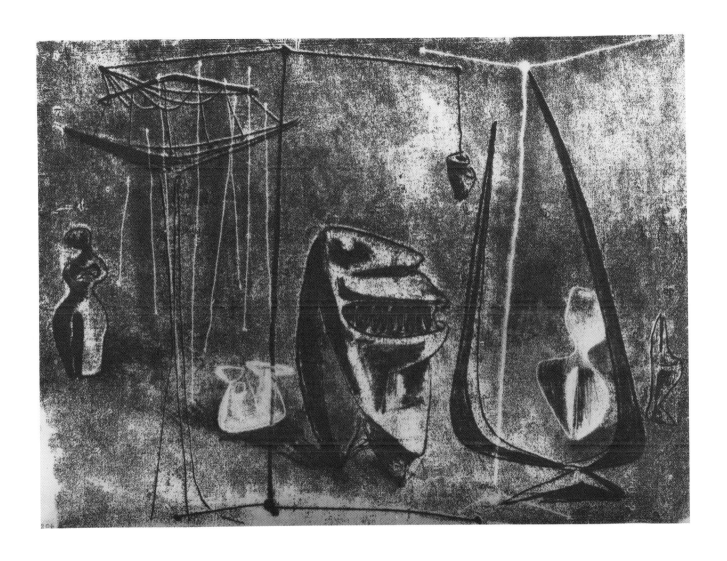

The 1950s

While some of the images of the 1950s relate more closely to nature than those of the forties, most of them remain nonobjective. Even accounting for the confusion that exists as a result of our tendency to associate what we see before us with what we know, as many as twenty-one of the thirty-two works reproduced here from the fifties can be considered in the strictly nonobjective category. As is pointed out in the discussion of the individual prints, seven of these are closely related to individual sculptures and several others contain drawings of what appear to be sculptural ideas. The fact that from 1953 on, Bertoia was engaged in the making of metal sculpture as his major occupation certainly affected, as it was affected by, his graphic work. Plates 26–28, for instance, are designs for sculpture based on the block-printed works of the forties; plates 34–36 show evidence of the effect of his work with stiff metal rods in the chair designs and small sculptures of the fifties; and plates 40 and 58 reveal the translation of motifs of mobility and the use of flexible wire from ink to metal and vice versa.

The nature to which some of the other works are close is, however, only minimally representative of what we see around us. Structures of vaguely human or animal resemblance stand and cast shadows, giving an impression of three-dimensional reality to their fantastic forms. Frequently these creatures are geometricized, as in the "swans" of plate 29 and the "dancers" of plates 49 and 50. Or they are rendered metallic and mechanical like the "robots" of plate 30 and the quasi-humans of plate 31. In only one case are we given a truly close resemblance to the human, and that is in the abstraction of a head of plate 48, which led directly to a small sculpture.[10]

Often the idea of landscape is suggested in these works by something as minimal as a broad band of granular ink indicating a ground line at the bottom of the print. Sometimes, as in the cognate plates 56 and 57, an indication is given of growth along the ground line, increasing its resemblance to reality. In the case of plates 42 and 43 we are encouraged to think of looking down on a realistically receding panorama with tall telephone poles casting long shadows across the land. Nature has certainly been the inspiration for the setting of many of these works but always it is treated with a vision either poetic or fantastic.

The graphics of the fifties are about evenly divided between those that present standing, and those that present floating, forms. As might be expected, the floating images, except for those that might have been intended to represent cosmic forces, are all nonrepresentational. With the floating lines and forms, as well as with many of the standing figures, there is a greater tendency in the fifties to print the image against a blank sheet of white paper and to use the granular textured ink for shading or contrast rather than as an overall background.

There is ample evidence of Bertoia's continuing fascination with aspects of negative and positive ambiguity in the heads, especially plate 47, as well as in plates 54 and 55 and the other cognate pairs of the fifties. The continued felicitous adaptation of negatives from a previous work to a totally new print is seen to advantage in plates 36–39, 41, and 50–52.

Perhaps the most noticeable change is that the geometry of the forties dies out entirely during this decade except where it is used in the service of more whimsical ideas. The only block-printed works are those of the early fifties, which establish motifs for the structure of sculpture, as in plates 26–28, the first two of which use essentially square modules. The triangles of former days survive into the late fifties but only in open constructions, as in plates 49–53, which use fan-shaped linear triangles to produce visions of fantasy.

Some of the images of the late fifties—those done after Bertoia's return from his 1957 European trip—take on a new dimension. They exhibit larger, bolder, and more powerful images than those of the forties. Most probably those prints done on the Italian watermarked paper (plates 30, 42, 43, 47, and 48) date from this period.

Some of the other bold works from the latter part of the decade include plates 29, 52, and 54–57. It is possible to postulate an influence from the strong, dramatic works of the Italian Renaissance, which Bertoia would have seen for the first time while visiting his homeland. Certainly, in these prints, contrasts are emphasized, there is a strong sense of drama, and the confident, powerful strokes of brush or stylus are expressive of kinetic energy.

Color, in Bertoia's prints of the fifties, becomes muted or monochromatic. Bright colors like those used in the textural block prints of the early forties disappear entirely. Except for plate 27 and scattered touches in plates 31 and 41, the primaries are dispensed with. The most frequently used colors in the fifties are red-brown, gray, and black, sometimes in combination but frequently monochromatically. This may have been a matter of expediency, as a great many graphics were done during the fifties along with a great deal of sculpture. Speed, as Bertoia indicated in his statement of 1976, was always important. It is a far speedier procedure to ink a plate with one color only than to use a variety of colors placed in particular areas of a design, requiring painstaking care in the placement of the color or the use of more than one plate.

The varieties and shapes of paper used by Bertoia in the fifties become much more standardized. Except for the group of works mentioned earlier as having been done on heavy watermarked paper, all except plate 39 were done on laid rice paper.[11] To be sure, not all of the laid paper is of the same type. Some of it was made with a narrower grid than other varieties and has yellowed over the intervening years. Five of the works reproduced here (plates 32–36) are printed on the narrower-grid paper and are all roughly the same size (ten by twenty-six inches) and are, therefore, all assumed to be from the early part of the decade. Later on, a finer grade of laid rice paper is adopted with a 1- or 1¼-inch grid. This has more or less standard measurements of twenty-four by thirty-nine inches, sometimes used whole by Bertoia but often split in half to achieve a twelve-by-thirty-nine-inch

measurement. Its first use in the prints published here dates from about 1953, but it is used much more frequently in the late fifties.[12]

Whereas in the forties many of the compositions could be considered from either a horizontal or vertical point of view, the horizontal format is definitely preferred in the fifties except for the group of works printed on the C. Miliani-Fabriano paper, all of which are vertically oriented. Unlike those of the forties, few of the compositions of the fifties could be looked at advantageously either way. The elongated horizontal makes its first appearance in the fifties, at first in small works measuring six by twelve or ten by twenty-six inches, culminating in works of such extended dimensions as six by twenty-four and twelve by thirty-nine inches. The latter, being the split size of the favorite laid paper of the latter part of the decade, becomes more and more extensively used. The unusual shape of these extended horizontals seems to have satisfied Bertoia's requirements in a great many works and produced some extraordinarily effective compositions.

Plate 26 (1950–54)

Colored inks and metallic ink on laid rice paper
Image: 14½ × 17; *paper:* 19½ × 24

Here, Bertoia uses the familiar stamping technique with
three different sizes of squares, but they have been
stamped from the back of the paper, which was laid over
a plate inked rather dully with gray and brown inks. A
few short vertical lines give the impression of a supporting and connecting structure while, at bottom, a sweep of
the hand produced a granular streak as a base for the
standing screen. Apparently, the bottom ground was an
afterthought as it contains within it a negative impression
of the lower part of the screen itself. The print was apparently pulled, then laid down again just off register before
hand pressure was applied in order to obtain this effect.
Also after the print was pulled, some of the squares were
overstamped with silver ink which gives glitter here and
there, especially at the corners of the units—a reminder
of the surface gleam of the object for which this drawing
was a study. Photographs exist of a small (thirty-six-inch-
high) sculpture screen of 1954 that almost exactly parallels this monographic.

Plate 27 (1952–55)

Colored inks on yellowed laid rice paper
Image: 4¹³⁄₁₆ × 11¹⁵⁄₁₆; *paper:* 5⅝ × 11¹⁵⁄₁₆

A combination of techniques was used here. Squares
and rectangles were stamped directly on the face of the
paper in red-orange, brown, blue, yellow, and green.
Then the paper was laid over a brown-inked plate, from
which a granular impression was received all around the
edges and, spottily, across the center. Vertical ruled lines
were drawn from top to bottom edge of the plate, spaced
regularly, about one inch apart. Other fine lines were
drawn freehand in the form of open squares, rectangles,
and parallelograms around or overlapping the opaque
stamped forms. The forms and freehand lines are scattered across the image but the design is held together by
the ruled verticals. At top and bottom the white grid of
the laid paper can be seen through the granular background. This tiny drawing is related to the St. Louis Airport screen done in 1955.[13] Although it is not a precise
plan for that sculpture commission, it is one of many
small studies exhibiting the openness, square modules,
and bright colors that characterized the final forty-foot-
long enameled-metal sculpture.

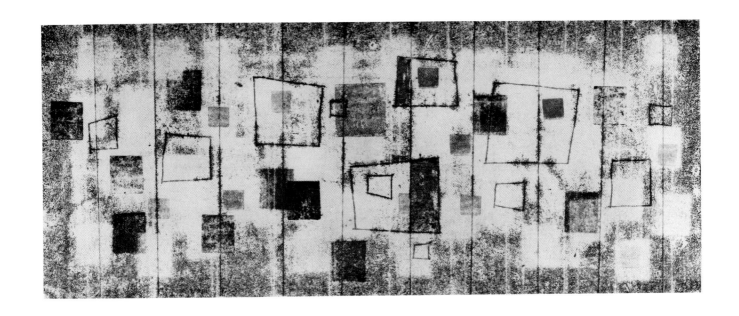

Plate 28 (1950s)

Printer's ink (black) on rice paper
Image: 5 × 22¼; paper: 9¼ × 25

Bertoia did many sculpture screens throughout his career
and was always particularly concerned with scale and
environment for each individual commission. Plate 28
once again adopts the stamping technique from the back
to represent in black ink a series of eight different ideas
for the structural components of such metal screens. Each
of the eight uses a different module, and various implements were used to suggest these in the drawing: tiny
stamped wood blocks for the squares, possibly pencil
erasers for the circles, a fine pointed stylus for the vertical
rods, and a sharp instrument (which put tiny holes in the
paper) for the flecks. Each unit shows some indication of
its structural support as it marches across the long horizontal like a decorative banner on parade.

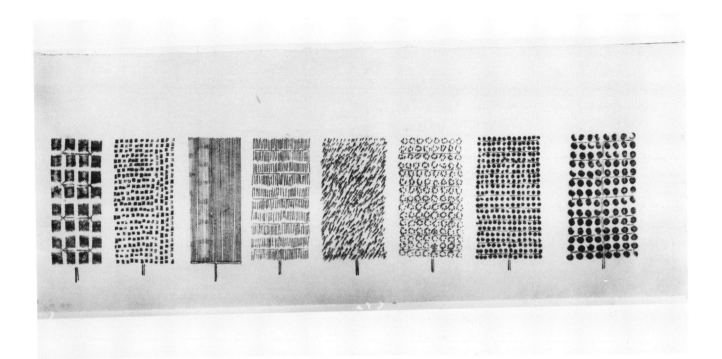

Plate 29 (1950s)

Colored inks on laid rice paper
Image: 11 × 24; *paper:* 12¼ × 25⅛

Four isolated forms having similar properties stand (or
sit) on a dark blue granular ground above which is blank
space met by delicate vertical sweeps of ink shading
downward from blue to black to brown. The properties of
the four forms give them the general appearance of
swans. They have large bodies or wing structures from
which proceed very long, thin neck projections ending in
small enlargements of a roughly triangular nature, two of
them curvilinear, the others angular. The largest "swan"
at left is reflected in the direction and shape of its head
and neck by a smaller figure at extreme right. The body
of the latter, however, resembles two wing structures on
either side of a single standing cone shape topped by a
much smaller inverted cone receiving and balancing a
projecting phallic object that separates the wings (the balancing of a large object on a slender fulcrum was typical
of Bertoia's sculptures of the late forties and early fifties).
The two central "swans" are seen in profile, necks stretch-
ing to the right. They are considerably more angular in
body, neck, and head, though each reflects the particulars
of one of the more curvate pair.

All figures were drawn from the back of the paper and
were shaded with rapid, often crisscrossing, strokes of the
stylus. There is a suggestion of cast shadows. The plate
must have been freshly cleaned before inking as there are
no negative images.

In spite of the isolation of the figures, there is a kind of
story dialogue set up between the neck-stretching
"swans," which seem to squawk at a recalcitrant sibling
while mother hen sits calmly by. The whimsically geome-
trized forms add much to the comic fantasy.

Plate 30 (1957–59)

Black and brown-black ink on paper watermarked
"C. Miliani-Fabriano"
Image: 21¼ × 17½; *paper:* 22 × 17⅝

Here, the drawn and shaded figures look like robots, two
of them humanized to the extent of being given a neck
and head. The heads are distinguished by two vertical rectangular openings in the one and by three horizontal slits
in the other placed in typical eye and mouth positions.
The two humanized robots stand at left—tall, slender,
and angularly jointed in several places as though capable
of some kind of jerky movement. Their short, stubby
counterparts at right are equipped with flat table tops
each containing two short projections.

   Each figure stands on its own square or angular base.
Cast shadows are indicated in the black ink through
which can be seen, at the bottom of the heavy paper, the
watermark as well as a few negative angular lines and
shapes from a cognate. The chiaroscuro emphasizing the
angularity of the forms was accomplished by the more
usual Bertoia method of rubbing with the thumb or a
stick from the back. The ink is black throughout except at
the left edge where it shades almost imperceptibly into
brown and where a tall negative robotic figure from a previous print emerges ghostlike to join the others.

Plate 31 (1950s)

Colored inks on laid rice paper
Image: 22¼ × 37¾; *paper:* 24 × 39

The isolation of the swans and the robots of plates 29
and 30 is repeated, to some extent, here, where the largest figure, just left of center, is made more human than
the others in its roundness and its large, skirted trunk and
armlike appendages, topped by a long neck supporting
an inverted, truncated pyramid for a head. This figure is
turned in three-quarters view to appear to communicate
with another, much less human, structure facing it. The
sense of isolation is diminished by this confrontation as
well as by the grouping of the three forms on the right
and the four on the left. The latter figures are simpler
than the major one in that each consists of a long, tapered stem supporting a broad form at its top. The shapes
of the tops vary from circular to oval to trapezoidal and
are given the appearance of three-dimensionality through
shading and cast shadows.[14] The effect of a dialogue is
even stronger here than in plate 29, but here it occurs
among a futuristic race of people.

The ghostly negative just right of center with its long,
tapered stem and flattened oval head (reminding one of a
Cycladic idol) reveals the existence of a cognate as do the
few negative lines at left and far right. The ghostly figure
was produced by pressure of a brayer on the back of the
paper, as a straight edge of dark ink to the right of the
"ghost" attests. All positive figures are in black ink
against a background that is white except where broad
sweeps of the hand produced light mottled areas. Horizontal streaks of reddish ink appear at left in the ground
area, while touches of red, orange, and yellow in granular
texture illumine parts of the forms. Spotty irregularities
giving an added textural effect throughout many of the
inked areas may be due to dust or bits of old dried ink on
the glass plate. (See also color plate.)

Plate 32 (1950s)

Colored inks on laid rice paper
Image: 7½ × 25½; paper: 10¼ × 25¾

This is one of many monographics done in the early fifties on yellowing paper one of whose dimensions measures more than double the other. Although a few of these are treated as verticals, the composition of most, like this one, is meant to be read horizontally. In this case its horizontality is emphasized by the repetitive linear treatment involving both negative and positive parallels as well as by the fact that the plate, the edges of which are clearly seen, was considerably shorter even than the paper. The parallels are a carryover of the "electrical circuitry" seen in plates 13 and 14 done in the late 1940s. Here, it is arranged without elaboration against an irregular mottled background, giving a textural contrast to the smoothly flowing lines.

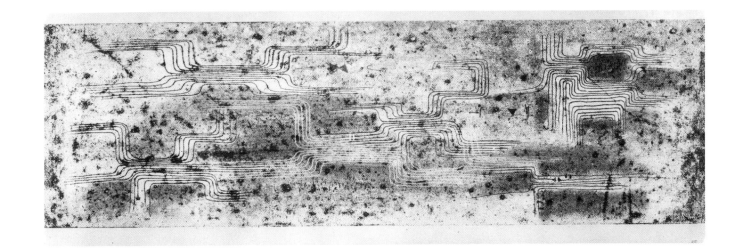

Plate 33 (1950s)

Gray and brown ink on laid rice paper
Image: 6⅞ × 24; paper: 10¼ × 25¾

This monographic is printed in approximately the same size and on the same kind of now yellowing rice paper as plate 32. Here, the background is blank paper and all lines are positive in charcoal gray ink. The design consists of a small blank ellipse at center which is encircled by three and a partial fourth ellipse of gradually increasing size, each placed slightly askew of the one which preceded it. Each ellipse is connected to the one next in size by repeated angled straight lines so that together they seem to form an asymmetrical spiral. At the outer edge similar lines angle off toward the unknown, a designation which is not inappropriate, as the formation resembles nothing so much as a galaxy like the Milky Way floating through space. The angled lines serve to give an effect of whirlwind motion while the elliptical void at center suggests the possibility of vortex action.[15] Drawn with fine lines of great delicacy and precision, the composition suggests powerful forces in action.

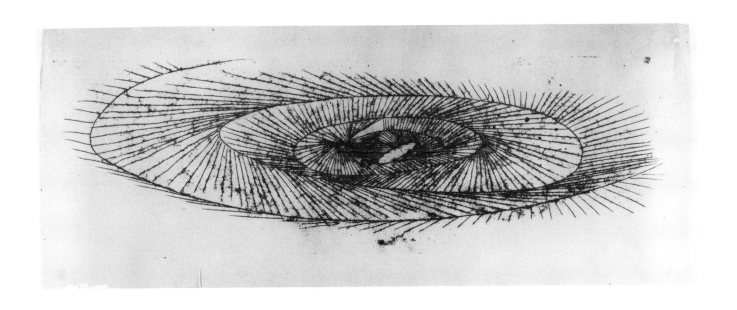

Plate 34 (1950s)

Black and brown inks on laid rice paper
Image: 25⅛ × 7½; *paper:* 25⅞ × 10⅛

Plate 35 (1950s)

Black and brown inks on laid rice paper
Image: 25 × 7½; *paper:* 25¾ × 10⅜

These two prints are a cognate pair done about 1950 on the same (yellowing) elongated paper, used this time vertically. The composition combines straight lines emanating from ellipses (in the manner of plate 33) with others radiating from single points. However, unlike the floating galaxy, it is eminently sculpturesque. The image in brown and black ink on plate 34 is one of a delicate construction that stands on tiny ball feet and rises to considerable height in balanced stages of airy cages. There are two branches of the structure at bottom, which interconnect at several points in the central area where lines converge, separating again to join at a single arc at the top. The delicacy becomes even more apparent in the cognate (plate 35), with its reversal of light and dark. A few new positive lines have been added here especially toward the top to further clarify the structure.

A three-foot sculpture, similar but not identical to these prints, is in the possession of the artist's widow (figure 5). As it is made of smooth brass rods and wires, the gleam of the metal contrasts with the softness of its shadow thrown against a wall. The sculpture can be dated ca. 1956.

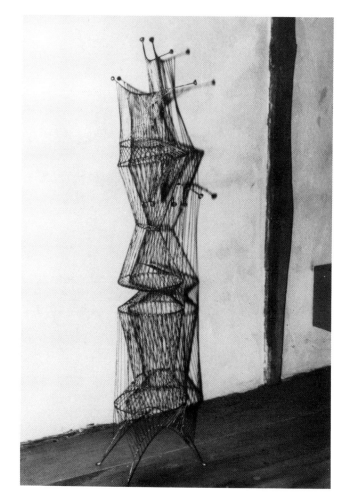

Figure 5. Untitled wire sculpture (ca. 1956), ht. 33 in. Collection of Brigitta Bertoia.

Plate 36 (1950s)

Gray and red-brown ink on laid rice paper
Image: 7½ × 25; paper: 10½ × 25½

Several versions of the sculptural idea in figure 5 (page
124) can be seen in this monographic, which adapts the
familiar elongated format to a series of individual variations on a theme. The inclusion of negative images from
the residue of a previous print brings to ten the number
of structures seen here, the positive additions overlapping
and interweaving with the negative to create a continuous composition. The two positive figures on the left deal
with random placement of lines representing metal rods
in the building of an open structure, a sculptural concept
that came to fruition for Bertoia in the late fifties and sixties. It should be noted that in spite of a sensation of
floating forms (the result of the absence of a ground line),
most of these figures have been provided with tiny ball
feet, an indication that they are meant to represent standing constructions. The plate from which this print was
made was covered in its upper portion with gray-black
ink shading into red-brown over the lower half with
greatest intensities at the horizontal center.

Plate 37 (1950s)

Red-brown and gray ink on laid rice paper
Image: 2½ × 23⅜; paper: 5⅝ × 23⅝

This is one of the best of a group of monographics probably done in the early fifties whose images have the unusual dimensions of only 2½ inches high by nearly 24
inches wide. The shape is so difficult to handle that these
prints have been preserved creased in half, inside heavy
paper folders, or framed in groups of six or more, one
above the other.

In this work color alternates between gray and red-
brown in vertical granular swaths, one color merging into
the other across the long horizontal. The spotty texture,
especially on the right side, is probably the result of ex-
cess turpentine but it is exactly the kind of accidental effect that pleased Bertoia very much (figure 6). All draw-

Figure 6. Detail of plate 37.

ing is partially obscured by the background texture; most
is negative, from one or more cognates of the same dimensions, on which a number of linear structures were
described one by one across the page. Very few positive
lines have been added, and these mostly give direction or
emphasis where prior structures were especially nebulous.

The effectiveness of the composition lies in the sensation of softness conveyed by the granular background
and the rhythm of the ghostly images as they progress
from side to side in slow and lyrical motion.[16] Whether

the linear structures here are standing or floating in space
is immaterial, as they all seem to disintegrate in the wa-
tery haze that surrounds them.

Plate 38 (late 1950s)

Printer's ink on laid rice paper
Image: 11 × 37½; *paper:* 12 × 39

Done in the late fifties in monochromatic gray-black ink, this print is among the first shown in this catalog to use what became a favorite paper size in the sixties, twelve by thirty-nine inches—attenuated dimensions far from the "golden mean." Eight separate linear structures are spaced across the long horizontal sheet, which has received the imprint of a previous drawing by selective hand or brayer rubbing. Some of the positive structures were either added to the surface of the print or drawn from the back on a second plate.

Four of the positive drawings either are placed against a totally blank background or take little or no cognizance of the negatives behind them. The others use positive line combined at times with shadowing to create new illusionistically three-dimensional structures based on the old. Most of the structures depicted use repetitive line fanning radially from a point or paralleling a contour. Two of them, however, show a new development introduced in Bertoia's sculptures of the late fifties and sixties involving a seemingly helter-skelter assemblage of rods such as those he had been using for his chairs.[17] Like the sculptures they reflect, the structures here exist as a kind of volume with little or no density as it is made up of space (air) interwoven with line (metal rod or wire).

The delicate precision of the positive lines throughout the print contrast effectively with the scattered ghostly images of the cognate amid the soft-edged granular texture of background passages. The effect is alternately soft and sharp, as images seem to come in and out of focus almost imperceptibly. The sweeping negative arcs of circles, like soap bubbles floating across the horizon, give a decorative cohesiveness to the composition which might otherwise be merely a disjointed series of studies (figure 7).

Figure 7. Detail of plate 38.

An earlier work in this series was exhibited in the invitational "Drawings USA 1961" exhibition at the St. Paul Art Center (now the Minnesota Museum of Art). Its basic ghostly circles reveal a third common cognate, but it contains a completely different set of positive representations, several of which appear in plate 38 in the negative.

Plate 39 (1950s)

Brown and green ink on rice paper
Image: 6 × 20; paper: 9 × 24

The concept of lines placed randomly, every which way, already seen to some extent in plates 36 and 37 as it began to be applied to sculptural structure by Bertoia, may derive from works of the late forties like plate 16. There, thin, shadowed verticals are crisscrossed at center by delicate, angled horizontals that seem to float in space. Here, shadowed, angled verticals of varying lengths are scattered over the dark brown- and green-inked background. They are connected by more delicate, angled horizontals in a network of lines that draws together the whole rambling structure. Many white (negative) verticals and other fine, white lines are also seen, some scratched out of the inked plate before the paper was laid down, some from a cognate. The use of shadowing gives many of the positive lines the look of three-dimensionality.

The linear structure, which resembles a split-rail fence or corral, seems to float on the granular surface, which is inked more heavily in some areas than in others. The many small, irregular white spots, each centered by a dot of ink, especially those scattered across the bottom of the print, are the result of flecks of dried ink deposited on the glass by the inking brayer.

Plate 40 (1953–54)

Colored inks on laid rice paper
Image: 21½ × 38; paper: 24 × 39

Elements similar to those used in the last print are here
transformed by shortening and thickening the angled verticals and making the structure of horizontal lines even
more delicate. The vertical strokes here probably were
made by the flat ends of balsa-wood sticks. They scatter
randomly across the center of this large print, seeming to
tumble like snowflakes from a cloud, a nature reference
suggested by the broad, soft-edged, horizontal band of
granular-textured ink that defines the underside of such a
suggested form. At lower left is a tiny replica of the major
elements of the larger design above. Translated into small
sheet-metal plaques strung on stiff wires, designs such as
this were put into sculptural reality in 1954 in the form of
wall- and ceiling-suspended works.[18] With regard to the
"cloud" sculptures and the monographics from which
they were descended, Bertoia said, "My intention was to
do something that did not have an edge. I made an effort
to fill out, to explode."[19]

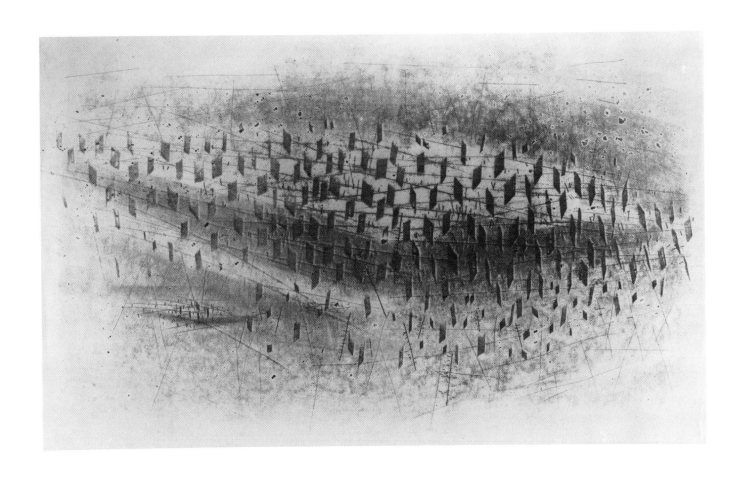

Plate 41 (1953–54)

Colored inks on laid rice paper
Image: 17½ × 37½; *paper:* 24 × 39

No sculpture exists nor could exist based on this print, a large monographic whose varied linear units float on the paper unconnected by any stabilizing framework. The elements are similar to those seen in the previous two plates: angled verticals of various thicknesses and degrees of sharpness, softness, and delicacy. Two cylinderlike slanted verticals almost one-inch thick dominate the center echoed by another pair of much shorter lines barely one-sixteenth of an inch thick to their immediate left. Whatever instrument was used to make the central pair produced a round-ended, softly shaded stroke that gives them the appearance of three-dimensional floating fence posts or telephone poles. The length and relative softness of these verticals is in contrast to the short, sharp-edged delineations made, like their counterparts in the previous print, with the angled flat edges of balsa-wood sticks. Other lines of greater or lesser thickness and intensity float across a broad, white-flecked, horizontal band of color or scatter from it at a downward angle from right to left.

Color and its method of application are important here. The glass plate, which had already been used at least once before, was inked with blue-black around the edges, then red-brown, and yellow near the center, each color merging into the next. Portions of the yellow overlay the blue and the brown producing brief green and orange touches. The broad horizontal band, which picks up ghostly elements from a previous work, was created by rubbing the back of the paper with the side of the hand, thus producing the soft, granular texture that Bertoia admired. It is this band that reveals the progression of colors on the inked plate. All lines, also drawn from the back, pick up in somewhat greater intensity (because of the greater pressure employed) the same colors. A color harmony results which unifies the scattered composition and emphasizes the contrasting effects of softness and sharpness that animate the work. It is one of the most poetically evocative—mysterious, yet satisfying—of Bertoia's prints. Along with plate 40 it became part of a slide presentation of fifty monographics made up in 1955 and called *Graphic Poem.*[20] (See also color plate.)

Plate 42 (1957–59)

Black ink on paper watermarked "C. Miliani-Fabriano"
Image: 19½ × 15½; paper: 22 × 17¾

This monographic, along with plate 43, can be assigned
with some assurance to the late fifties, as the watermarked paper on which they are printed is believed to
have been brought back by Bertoia from his trip to Italy
in 1957. They are related works, both being vertical compositions in black ink on the same kind and size of paper,
using angled, vertical motifs similar to those recently discussed. In the first print, rows of randomly spaced and
variously angled thin vertical lines proceed in zigzag fashion from lower left to the top of the page. In their progress they either follow or cross small areas of granular
black ink that diminish in size and intensity, just as the
lines diminish in length and distinctness, as they rise. The
verticals are further given the appearance of standing
structures receding into the distance by the addition of
shorter lines angled downward to the left from their
bases, an indication of cast shadows. Many of the tall verticals are crossed by short, more or less horizontal, lines,
like the crossbars of telephone poles. There is some indication in the foreground area of negative lines from a
prior print, contributing an effect of sunlight streaming
past long shadows on the ground.

The white spot around a fleck of dried ink at upper left
is, of course, accidental. Here, it detracts from, rather than
adds to, the general effectiveness of the composition.

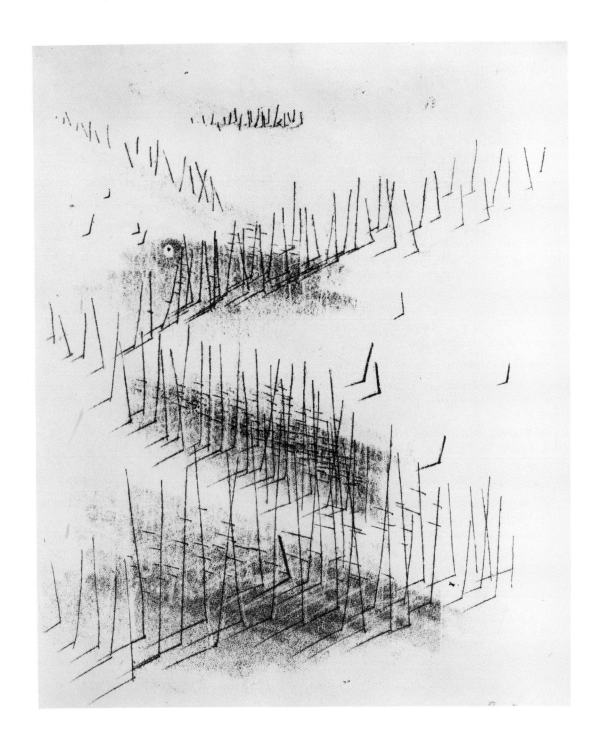

Plate 43 (1957–59)

Black ink on paper watermarked "C. Miliani-Fabriano"
Image: 18 × 16¼; *paper:* 22 × 17¾

The impression of fence posts and telephone poles march-
ing across the countryside is confirmed here, where some
of the slanted verticals are thicker and the crossbars are
limited to one per pole, with dots reminiscent in their
placement of the ceramic insulators for electrical connec-
tions. It seems clear that this work was produced in tan-
dem with plate 42 and that they derived from ideas expressed in earlier works, such as plates 41, 39, and
possibly even plate 16 and the vertically balanced sculptures of the late forties. Such a progressive development
may or may not have originated with an observation of
the natural world, but it corroborates a statement of his
creative philosophy once made by Bertoia: "If an idea is
valid, it has been with me for many years."[21]

Plate 44 (1952–56)

Colored inks on laid rice paper
Image: 7½ × 12¼; paper: 8½ × 12¼

In spite of its subdued colors (dark brown and red-brown with just a few very delicate touches of yellow), one feels this monographic deserves a title such as EXPLOSION!

The composition consists of lines and flecks, essentially the same elements used in plates 39–41 but with quite a different effect. Here they are made with a variety of instruments and in ways which, through kinesis, affect our reaction to the image. The delicate curved lines at lower right appear to have been done somewhat deliberately and are carefully paralleled. The thin, straight lines on the left, perhaps done with the same implement, are more random and were accomplished more hurriedly, giving a feeling, therefore, of urgency. The large flecks scattered all around the edges are from quick, hard strokes of a blunt instrument done almost angrily. They match in expressiveness the small, sharp ticks of a finer point that accumulate in great numbers, especially just left of center.[22] The background comes from hand, thumb, and finger pressure. Some of the small white lines and strokes may have been wiped from the plate with sticks or a cloth or, more likely, they are the residue of a prior print. There is some indication, as well, of shadowing, especially of the short lines at upper right.

The whole, however nebulous its structure, gives a marvelous evocation of explosive energy—the big bang in space that created the universe.

492

Plate 45 (1952–56)

Colored inks and powdered metal on laid rice paper
Image: 11 × 25; *paper:* 12⅛ × 25¼

Characteristics similar to those in plate 44 are seen here
in an elongated horizontal format that helps to keep the
explosions more contained. The basic ink colors are gray
and red-brown, and the background area is generally
considerably more dense but with bright white spaces
surrounding each of the four explosions of different sizes
and intensities. The density of the background is augmented somewhat as a result of powdered metal sprinkled over the surface, creating a golden sheen when the
paper is held at certain angles, but which does not photograph well. The four, roughly circular structures are made
of random, crisscrossing lines interspersed with tiny
flecks and shaded to give a spherical impression. In the
large sphere, especially, some of the lines appear to radiate out from center while the flecks are placed at their
tips in such a manner as to give an effect of slowly turning motion to the loose structure.

Compared with plate 44 this print has a much calmer
appearance, as though it described a further step in the
evolution of the universe. Its use of lines and flecks also
comes close in appearance to the realization in three-
dimensional form with metal rods and wires that Bertoia
achieved in the 1950s, a program that "began almost
purely as a concept—a total abstraction almost. But then
it began to take place as a play of two infinities, . . . an
exercise of mind."[23] Such sculptures were sometimes
stemmed works referred to as "bushes," "dandelions,"
and "trees"; others became wall- or ceiling-suspended
"clouds."[24]

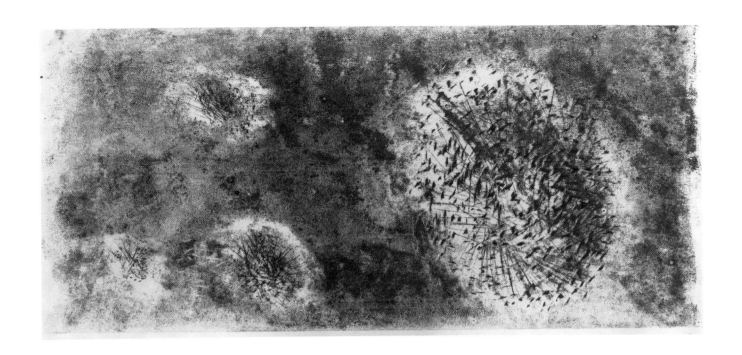

Plate 46 (1950s)

Brown ink on laid rice paper
Image: 11 × 23½; *paper:* 12³⁄₁₆ × 25¼

In the late fifties and throughout the sixties, Bertoia's graphics often become very closely allied to his sculptures. Whether of an experimental nature or more prosaically descriptive, they combine both line and form in concept and technique. Plate 46 appears at first glance to be a layout for cutting sheet-metal patterns for parts to be assembled into a construction. On closer inspection, however, none of the seven squares (representing sheets of metal?) lined up across the top of the print exactly fits any grouping of the large pieces shown at bottom, and several (the two at right in particular) seem totally unrelated to those below. The sculpture for which it was done, if there was one, is unknown today. This graphic is a simple line drawing in brown ink with handwritten notations readable from the back. Aside from the numbering of the horizontally elongated shapes, the notations cryptically indicate either "phone" or "plane" under the small shape at left, "accordion type expansion" under the larger shape, and "interlocking of forms" accompanying the four irregular shapes just right of center.

What is remarkable about this graphic is that although it clearly is a working drawing of the most utilitarian kind, it nevertheless produces a most pleasing effect based on aesthetic principles of unity, variety, and balance. The forms represented are unique, and they are arranged (without forethought, it would seem) according to an innate sense of spatial relationships.

Plate 47 (1957–58)

Colored inks on paper watermarked "C. Miliani-Fabriano"

Image: 22 × 17⅝; *paper:* same dimensions

In 1957–58 Bertoia did a series of at least eighteen experimental studies of heads, which culminated in one of the very few representational sculptures he ever did. The studies are all highly abstracted. Each takes a different approach, and often a different technique is employed.

The present monographic is one of the most abstract of all, being barely recognizable as a head by the supporting neck at its base and its relationship to the other works in the series. Whereas at first glance it seems to have used trapezoidal blocks of varying dimensions stamped or pressed on the surface (as in his earliest prints of 1943), the actual technique was totally different. It involved some transfer of ink from a glass plate, but most of the sharp-edged forms were created by direct application of the brayer to the surface of the paper. The general colors are blue-black, brown, and red-brown. Linear accents were added in black, yellow, and orange. A cubist effect is achieved of overlapping transparent planes. At times it seems a flat pattern; at other times it appears clearly three-dimensional. (See also color plate.)

Plate 48 (1957–58)

Black ink on paper watermarked "C. Miliani-Fabriano"
Image: 22⅛ × 17¾; *paper:* same dimensions
Collection of Mr. Raymond Leight, Jr., West Point,
Pennsylvania

Much closer than the previous work to the culminating
metal sculpture is this graphic, which uses random crisscrossing lines to achieve its effect. These were eventually
translated into brazed rods welded together to form an
airy volume in the shape of a head.[25] The monographic
was partly drawn directly on the glass plate. Many lines
scratched into the wet ink are clearly visible, and some of
the dark lines may have been painted with a brush. Others were added from the back after the paper was laid on
the inked surface. The ink here is black and the paper is
heavy Italian watermarked paper, the same paper used
for all the head studies. In this print its texture augments
the granular effect of the shaded areas. The wiped areas
and scratched-out lines provide highlights and animation
for this lively presentation of a human head. Its constructed metal counterpart adds another dimension to
those of Gabo, Pevsner, Gonzalez, and Picasso done earlier in the century.

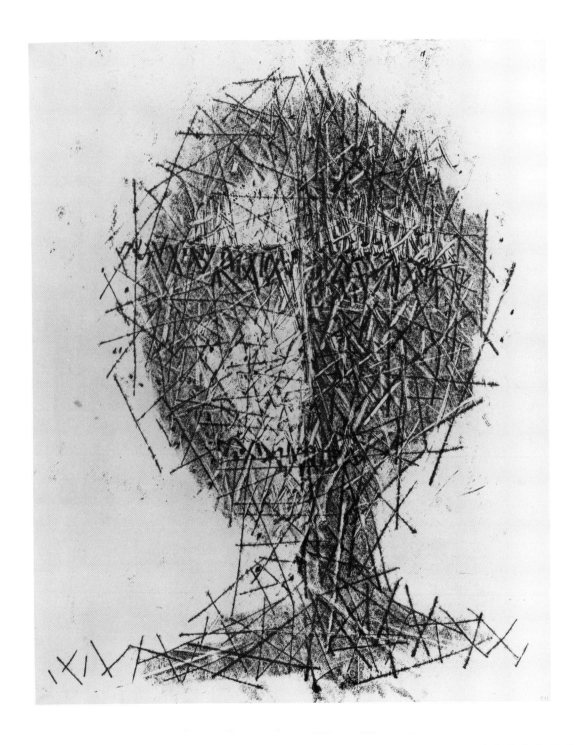

Plate 49 (1954–56)

Colored inks on laid rice paper
Image: 22⅜ × 38¼; *paper:* 24¼ × 39

Some graphics originating in the fifties are characterized by the representation of complex forms made from linear triangles. The triangles are formed of radiating lines fanning out from a single point. Each triangle is then joined with one or more similarly formed, either at one of its points or on a flat side. In this way they grow into jointed figures often bearing a vague resemblance to human beings—frequently one has two "legs" or "arms" and a single appurtenance at the top that might serve as a head. In a way, this is an adaptation of the geometric precision of the forties to ideas of greater fantasy.

Such figures are sometimes seen in a landscape setting, as in the present work, where a broad horizontal band of negative (white) lines establishes a ground line and acts as a barrier fence to the beyond as it passes through the blue-black and dark red ink. The fence is "electrified" by many tiny vertical lines, both negative and positive, scattered throughout. Two large figures of the type just described stand in front of this horizontal grid. The figure on the left, taller and sparer than its partner, is drawn in lines of blue-black ink at top and bottom shading to red-black at center whereas the more voluptuous figure on the right shades to green in the middle, the result of yellow ink overlaying the blue in that area. These are powerful figures more than seventeen inches tall on a sheet of paper measuring twenty-four by thirty-nine inches. The lines that make them are straight, forceful, and strongly colored. The figures stand on small, triangular feet dominating their space and, because of the directional thrust of many of the triangles that make up their forms, they appear to move to the left in a kind of slow, ritual dance or procession. For more regarding the technique of this graphic, see the discussion of plate 50.

Plate 50 (1954–56)

Colored inks on laid rice paper
Image: 22¼ × 38½; paper: 24¼ × 39

The negatives of the two figures of plate 49 are seen here in a cognate. The technique of these two graphics is very puzzling. That the horizontal band in plate 49 was picked up from a previous plate is attested by the barely visible negative sunburst at its extreme right. The colors of the two figures are intense and differ sufficiently from their immediate surrounding background ink to make one believe they were added from a separate plate. This seems especially likely since the background fence does not appear in plate 50. However, a comparison of the location of spots of dried ink on the two prints seems to indicate that the whole of plate 49 was reused as the basis for plate 50. It is possible to reink a plate lightly and still retain enough of the shadowy image of the previous drawing to register on a second print, and this may very well have been done. Some wiping obviously occurred as the circle in the middle and the rectangle at right witness. The sunburst and the small positive figures may have been produced through the use of another plate. A slide exists of a third print in this series in which all of the elements of plate 50 appear in the negative along with additional positive figures.

Intensified shading, the sunburst, and several tiny triangular figures (one of them particularly human) were added from the back along with a number of short, delicate verticals that serve to imply a grassy sward in the foreground. Additional lines in dark red ink were applied to the large figure on the right after the print was pulled to increase its appearance of articulation and three-dimensionality. Shadowing aids the impression of volume in the small structures, some of which look more like plant forms than humans.

This strange landscape is enlivened by the contrast between the large ghostly figures and the small sharply delineated ones. The starkness of the irregular circle surrounding the "sun" and the rectangle of light that frames the more human apparition on the right seem intrusions of reality in a dream world.

Plate 51 (late 1950s)

Black ink on laid rice paper
Image: 11 × 38½; *paper:* 12 × 39

A further development of the motif in plates 49 and 50, the linear triangles here are not used to build whimsically grotesque creatures who dominate a landscape but rather to construct the landscape itself.

   With the aid of one or more cognates, in monochromatic black ink, an impression is given of a fantastic city of the future whose buildings rise in majestic groups balanced on slender points much like modern cantilevered structures. Groups of forms in deep black ink rise higher than and contrast sharply with a shadowy group of structures in negative line from a previous print, establishing foreground-background relationships. The spaces between the triangles become important, especially in the group at left but also in the background structure where the spaces that had been white on a previous plate are now dark, though not, of course, as dark as the positive lines of the foreground. What is form in one becomes space in the other, and vice versa, in a play of negative against positive. Sweeps of granular gray ink of different intensities provide sky and ground, and some articulation is given to the latter by a few thin, angular lines.

   This extensive panoramic cityscape in elongated horizontal format is peopled by a number of tiny, dark verticals in scattered clusters with even tinier, angled lines at their bases to indicate cast shadows. Particularly notable are the sensitively handled asymmetric balance of the forms and spaces, as well as the wide variation in tonality. Together they have produced a print of exceptional quality.

Plate 52 (late 1950s)

Black ink on laid rice paper
Image: 11 × 38⅝; *paper:* 12 × 39

In horizontal elongation and monochromatic inking, plate 52 presents on its right-hand side structures similar to those of plate 51 but somewhat less precisely rendered. Complete with shadowy background, it appears also to represent a futuristic city and its surroundings, culminating in the foreground, near center, in a slightly askew monumental structure of linear triangles rising in stages to a radiant sphere at its apex like a huge sentinel or beacon. An effect of atmospheric perspective is created by the negative structures of the background standing out in relief against soft, dark swirls of granular textured ink simulating wind-swept clouds. The negative arcs and other notations adding to the effect of distance come from the same cognate used as a base for plate 38 (figures 8A and 8B).

Figure 9. Detail of plate 52.

strokes are thick, black, and heavy with the force of their making or scratched in with a fine point in nervous, erratic wispiness. At the far left spiraling lines and soft, echoing smudges spring upward from the conflagration below (figure 9). The semblance of a continuation of fore-

Figure 8A. Detail of plate 52.

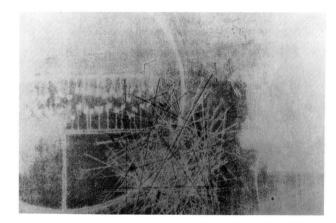

Figure 8B. Detail of plate 38.

Plate 52 changes character at left where precision gives way to complete chaos. Broad, dark, velvety strokes of ink at bottom erupt into a mushroom cloud of fine, sharp, dark lines surrounded by soft swirls. The image is explosive and expressive in the manner of plate 44. The

ground, horizon, and sky ties the explosive left half to the more serene and orderly right in an unpeopled panorama —a powerful evocation of a wasteland.

The tonality of this print is truly remarkable. It ranges from deep, velvety, lithographic blacks, through several

middle tones, to the palest of grays and, of course, white. At least two cognate plates were used, and a reinking was necessary after the cognate impressions were taken, in order to produce the darkest tones. There is also evidence of a few of the lines, particularly at lower left, drawn in ink on the back of the paper—but very few. Most of the drawing was made with implements that left no trace on the verso.

Both plates 51 and 52 exhibit, along with their fantasy, the new boldness that is characteristic of much of the work of the late fifties. While plate 51 is cool, clean, and precise, however, plate 52 has a baroque energy and emotional content that is totally lacking in the other. It is only at rare moments in Bertoia's oeuvre, which is generally so life-affirming, that we see images, like this one, that seem to concentrate on destruction. Of course, it is also possible to interpret the standing beacon as a symbol of survival and the arcs as rainbows over the civilization of the future. Interpretation, like beauty, is in the eye of the beholder, especially in a work like this, which probably grew in content as the drawing progressed.

Plate 53 (1956–57)

Gray and red-brown inks on laid rice paper
Image: 39⅛ × 11; *paper:* 39⅛ × 12

This monographic combines the linear-triangle figures with an effect achieved through the use of a new tool to produce a fantasy of esoteric spiritual content.[26] The elongated format being used vertically this time, the print contains in its lower section the negative image of a figure with its arms raised. Composed of fan-shaped triangles, the form is made to look human by the addition of positive triangles to form eye sockets and extend the legs. It has the appearance of some ritualized idol of prehistoric or future time and is vaguely connected by an elaborate headdress with another, less human form made up of similar elements drawn positively and precisely inside a blank oval. This latter, bifurcated figure has an elongated, diamond-shaped interior space partially filled by two straight lines, one descending and one rising from opposite points of the diamond. The two lines do not meet, but each has at its end a tiny circle from which short lines radiate toward its counterpart.

The lower (and larger) of the two forms is printed in gray ink and the upper in red-brown. Across the entire print, myriad fine lines sweep randomly in gray and red-brown ink surrounding and demarcating both a sidewise oval passing through the legs of the figure at bottom and the top-pointing egg shape that surrounds the upper figure. These lines were made through the use of a new tool, a stiff, wire dog brush.[27] They are effective in drawing together the elongated composition and in softening the angularity of the figures with their superimposed circular direction.

Much could be deduced about the mystic implications of this work. The idol (be it godhead, leader, or merely extraordinary being) raises its arms to receive inspiration from its own inner spirit (its soul?) or from another, truer spirit on high. The several indications of reaching up and out might allude to the aspirations of the human psyche.

The egg shapes—symbols of birth, the newborn, creativity—surround the two representations in different positions, perhaps signifying the changes undergone after impulses are received. Whatever the individual interpretation, it would have been neither confirmed nor denied by Bertoia, who preferred to let his works stand on their own. Their value lay, he felt, in stimulating thought and imagination, not in yielding a rigid meaning.

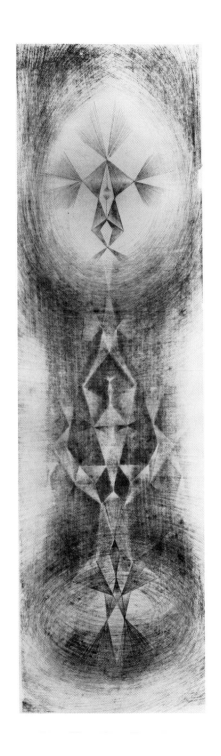

Plate 54 (1956–59)

Black and brown ink on laid rice paper
Image: 11 × 37¾; *paper:* 12 × 38¾
Collection of Mr. Raymond Leight, Jr., West Point,
Pennsylvania

Plate 55 (1956–59)

Black and brown ink on laid rice paper
Image: 11 × 38½; *paper:* 12 × 38⅞
Collection of Mr. Raymond Leight, Jr., West Point,
Pennsylvania

Work with the dog brush as drawing implement in the late fifties produced a series of prints in the elongated format that could be considered either vertically or horizontally. The two prints shown here were among Bertoia's earliest experiments with the implement.

In plate 54 a large bonelike image resembling a femur results from several dynamic sweeps of the brush across the back of the paper laid over a brown and black inked plate. Although the "bone" does not have firm outlines, the suggestion is nevertheless clear in the contrast between dark form and white background merging into white form shadowed with and surrounded by dark. In the one area, the brushed lines were used to indicate solid form, while in the other they indicate space, a follow-up of Bertoia's continuing interest in negative and positive ambiguities. Some of the curved lines and scumbling in the central area and elsewhere seem to have been added to the surface by short strokes of the inked wire brush.

Whether or not the idea of a thigh bone (with its round-headed knee joint and oblique hip joint) was in Bertoia's mind when he fashioned this image is unknown and immaterial. Certainly there was no attempt to accurately reproduce a part of the anatomy. The work is re-markable alone for the kinetic energy it displays, which reminds us of the power and vitality of the largest bone in the human body.

In the cognate, plate 55, Bertoia captured a somewhat nebulous negative image of the previous print by stroking the wire brush straight across the back of the paper laid on top of the ink remaining on the glass after plate 54 was pulled. Short strokes and scumbles were added again, some of them probably directly to the surface. The work lacks somewhat the force of its counterpart, having the effect of an X-ray image by comparison. As a pair, they are especially interesting in their double reversal of the negative-positive elements.

Plate 56 (late 1950s)

Black ink on laid rice paper
Image: 21½ × 38; paper: 24 × 39

Yet another pair of cognates, this and the following monographic create evocative images through use of the wire dog brush. These are works printed on the large-size laid rice paper used horizontally. Their size adds considerably to the effectiveness of the result. In the first print an enormous image appears like an elongated, irregularly shaped tire or doughnut in black ink against the stark white paper. The image originated with a single sweeping arm motion using the wire brush with considerable pressure from the back of the paper on a freshly cleaned and inked plate. The beginning and ending of the stroke are almost undetectable, so smoothly do they join to suggest a continuous motion. Another sweep of the brush with lighter pressure helps give an effect of three-dimensionality.

The resultant form has a strangely menacing quality, which is augmented by the addition of a ground line in granular texture, complete with grass and flowers. The hovering black form comes ominously close to but does not touch the ground. It has the effect of dynamic motion like some twisted cosmic tornado about to strike an unsuspecting planet. The strange undulations of the form combine with the kinetic quality of the brush work to produce a sense of foreboding. The stark black on white lends power to the image which has all the force of Goya's *Colossus* in abstract form.

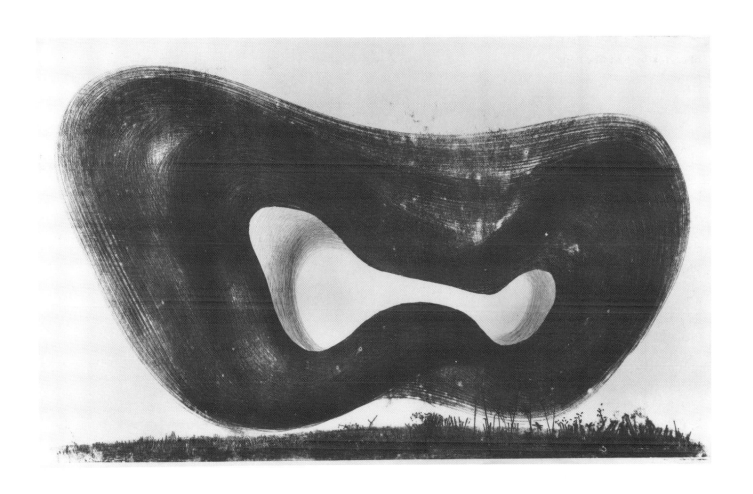

Plate 57 (late 1950s)

Black ink on laid rice paper
Image: 23 × 38⅜; paper; 24 × 39

This print contains the negative image of plate 56 including its grassy ground. The image was obtained in part by
brayer and hand pressure, but the wire brush was again
used in directional fashion around the perimeter and the
interior of the now ghostly form. The image seems more
like a cloud here as the sharp contours of the original
have been softened. However, the effect is equally dynamic and perhaps even more menacing, as though the
same cosmic phenomenon were taking place at night instead of in the clear light of day.

These last two wire-brush prints seem to be expressive
of anger or despair, moods infrequent to Bertoia. They
may reflect emotions at the sudden death of his good
friend, Hans Knoll, in the fall of 1955.

Plate 58 (late 1950s)

Gray and red-brown ink on laid rice paper
Image: 20½ × 30½; *paper:* 24 × 39

Bertoia also used the wire-brush implement in his search
for sculptural form of the most light-hearted kind. Here,
on a large sheet of laid rice paper, the image is of a hanging spray like the sculptures done in the late fifties and
sixties using flexible stainless-steel wire.[28] The dark wire-
brushed lines spray outward and either upward or downward in many strokes from a light center. Seen through
the red-brown lines are some white lines arched in a
more directly downward direction, the negative of a previous print. Tiny dots made with a pointed instrument
are scattered throughout, especially at the outer ends of
the lines, which also show evidence of strokes made by
pressing the end of the brush against the paper without
dragging it (figure 10). These emulate the pinpoints of

Figure 10. Detail of plate 58.

light created by the clipped ends of the steel wires. A
thin, straight line from the center to the top of the image
helps create the illusion of a light and airy suspended
sculpture that shimmers with delicate movement.

The 1960s

The distinction made among linear works, formal works, and works dealing with both line and form in the decades of the forties and fifties is of little use in the sixties. Perhaps as a result of the concentration on sculpture, all the graphics of this decade seem to have been conceived of in terms of form. There is little, if any, fantasizing such as had been indulged in earlier. The geometry of the forties is gone, but the clean precision of Bertoia's line lingers on while baroque irregularity plays an increasingly important role in his graphics as well as his sculpture. The graphic works of the sixties are tied very closely to the sculptures that occupied so much of his time during this decade. As a result of the tremendous increase in the number of commissions undertaken, as well as time spent on the musical program, there is a decline in the number of graphics produced.

Aside from the fact that there are considerably fewer of them, the most noticeable change in the images of the sixties has to do with their relationship to Bertoia's sculpture. Most of the prints are essentially working drawings for specific sculptures or sculptural ideas. They therefore take on a totally different character from the more graphically experimental and whimsical works of the previous two decades. This is true of all those printed here. Gone are the linear meanderings and the floating lines and flecks of the forties and fifties. The linear elements of the sixties are aids to construction, whether of airy, open forms, or more solid ones.

Many graphics of the sixties reveal inventive ideas along lines somewhat different from those encountered in previous decades. For the most part, these ideas have to do specifically with sculptural form. Some were intended to suggest new designs for metal rods and wire. Others investigate adaptations of form to types of industrially available metal products not previously adopted by Bertoia. In some cases, these would have required construction methods quite different from those Bertoia had been accustomed to using. There is no evidence that he pursued them beyond the graphic stage, however.

The bolder, more dramatic treatment of the image seen developing in the late fifties continues into the sixties, especially in plates 62–65. They contrast with the more delicate, poetically evocative images of earlier works. Strong curvilinear forms and constructions like those of plate 64 present themselves toward the end of the decade almost as a kind of reaction against the strict rectilinearity of such structures as those seen in plates 62 and 63. The sweeping curves of plate 64 have a baroque exuberance about them expressive of the joy of freedom and unrestrained growth.

Color in the 1960s turns often to black, occasionally varied with brown or blue. This is true of all but one of the works reproduced here. It may have been a matter of expediency, since most of the prints are working drawings of one kind or another. Even so, all but two do introduce a second color, albeit in a subdued manner. One work (plate 61), which is either a preparatory drawing or one done for record keeping, is the most elaborately colored of all in its painterliness. But even here there is no return to the vivid primaries of earlier days. The colors are in keeping with the working relationship of the graphics to their sculptural counterparts. The sculptures are often more colorful than the prints, what with brazing, gilding, polishing, and applications of patina or tiny touches of enamel on the metal.

The fine, translucent, laid rice paper adopted in the fifties is used exclusively in the sixties, especially in the large (twenty-four-by-thirty-nine-inch) size. A Masonite printing plate that Bertoia often used instead of glass in later years, was cut to fit this paper. The horizontal format is still preferred, especially, though not exclusively, the elongated horizontal. Four of the seven works shown here are on the large paper or the lengthwise torn or cut half of its purchased dimensions, a shape that continued to lend itself effectively to Bertoia's now more pragmatic images.

Plate 59 (1960s)

Blue and brown ink on laid rice paper
Image: 10½ × 37; paper: 12 × 39

Probably done early in 1962, this monographic depicts a number of structures recognizable in Bertoia's oeuvre of metal sculpture. At bottom left are four numbered forms that may have been intended as parts of a construction or as ideas for shapes for gongs.[29] Above these to the left is a standing sculpture of curved pipe sections joined side by side and two hanging "cloud" sculptures of the type made in the fifties and sixties of rods or wires welded together at random angles. In the center is a screen of sounding rods projecting vertically from a flat base. To the right are two standing works of the type made with flexible wires. In one, wires are attached in bunches at intervals projecting horizontally along both sides of a single, standing rod. In the other, the wires emanate in sunburst fashion from a central sphere atop a tall stem anchored in a heavy base. The latter is representative of sculptures that Bertoia originated in the late fifties, often referred to as "dandelions" because of their resemblance to the last phase of that flower's development.

The diversity of these sculptural ideas suggests that this print may have been a kind of minicatalog done as a record of types of work produced. Even in such a utilitarian compendium, the artist's considered judgment and innate sense of balance dictate the placement of each individual representation so that a unified composition is obtained. Essentially monochromatic, the print was made from a plate inked blue at the top, and brown at the bottom.

Plate 60 (1960s)

Black ink on laid rice paper
Image: 9⅛ × 25⅛; *paper:* same dimensions

Another group of five sculpture studies is seen in plate
60. Although the structures represented here seem unrelated to most of Bertoia's known three-dimensional
works, the depiction of pipe sections and obvious openings of one kind or another leads one to believe they may
have been experimental designs for fountain sculptures.
Essentially line drawings, the structures were shaded by
hand pressure to indicate the third dimension. There are
no afterimages or shadowing of consequence, although
the figure at right acquires a certain naturalism from the
spotty mottling derived from a prior print. Black ink
alone was the medium for this work. Like the numbered
elements on plate 59, practical notations appear here in
reverse writing as they were made, like the rest of the
drawing, from the back of the paper. To be read, even
from the back, the print must be held up to the light. The
notation beside the figure on the right reads "hydro-
formed, then cut section and weld rim."

Plate 61 (1962)

Colored inks on laid rice paper
Image: 8½ × 38; *paper:* 12 × 38⅞

Securely dated to the sixties, this graphic is a true mono-type, that is, it was painted on a plate using the dark-field method and then printed. It is related to the sculpture Bertoia considered his finest achievement—"unique in our age," is the way he put it. Most likely, the monotype was a preparatory graphic made for submission as a proposal for the untitled bronze screen completed and installed in time for the dedication of Washington's Dulles International Airport building in November 1962.[30] The project's unpredictable and slightly dangerous spill-casting technique, which Bertoia pioneered, is the sculptural equivalent of action painting. In spill-casting, as in the art of monotype, speed is essential. Like the *Fifty Drawings* of 1943, all nine panels of the thirty-six-foot-long bronze sculpture were cast in about twenty-four hours, after months of planning and preparation.[31]

Such is the nature of the process of manipulating molten bronze as it cools that the monotype as a preparatory plan would have been impossible to follow exactly. Comparison with a photograph of the completed sculpture indicates just how adaptable the sculptor had to be in the final casting. The deliberate indentation at the lower left edge of the monotype is a possible indication that it was made after the sculpture was completed rather than before. Could the monotypist have known that in the casting of one panel the bronze would pull away from its enclosing frame? On the other hand, Bertoia's experience may have made him aware of this possibility of the medium, and he may have worked to achieve such a result. In the actual sculpture panel, however, it appears at the upper, not the lower left.

For the monotype a plate was painted with green and red-brown inks, the colors of bronze and its patina, in summary notations of projected darks and lights. The image was further clarified by wiping and by manipulating the ink through the use of sticks and other implements in a manner not unlike that of the final casting. The separation of the nine panels was marked off on the print according to scale. Instead of ruled lines, an irregular scratching was used to minimally indicate the divisions and encourage transitional composition from one panel to the next. A few tiny highlights of bright red color were applied to emulate accents of polished bronze. There is also evidence of some positive linear additions, probably made from the back of the paper. An overall gray tonality, partially obscuring some of the light areas and darkening others in the manner of chiaroscuro, may have been added from a separate plate. If so, it was handled very carefully, as there is a single quite distinct plate line on all four sides of the print.

Like the sculpture it reflects, plate 61 creates an impression of the primeval forces that affected the surfaces of the planets during the formation of the universe—a further step in the evolutionary process of the heavenly bodies, in which Bertoia had been interested since the 1940s. In this regard it is especially interesting to note that the first photographs of the surface of the moon, which brought awareness of such phenomena into general cognizance and which resemble this monotype and its sculpture to a remarkable degree, were not made until the landing of Apollo five years later. (See also color plate.)

Plate 62 (1964)

Black and brown ink on laid rice paper
Image: 11 × 38¼; *paper:* 12 × 38¾

Plate 62 is one of several done for the 1964 Minneapolis sculpture called *Sunlit Straw.*[32] The sculpture is a gigantic standing structure forty-six feet long and fourteen feet high, made of brazed steel rods welded together in a seemingly haphazard manner. As the preliminary drawing indicates, it is a follow-up on the earlier ideas of repetitive and random placement of line. In the monographic, short, straight lines of varying thickness are grouped in fanlike images and jut out at all angles, crisscrossing their way across the elongated horizontal. The rigid linear structure is lightened by dots and flecks sprinkled throughout. In the sculpture these were translated into brightly colored, shiny, enameled pieces that contrast with the dry texture and golden color of the rods like spectrum-filled dewdrops or jewels fallen on a bed of straw. The print was realized from a plate randomly inked with red-brown and black, without additional color.

Plate 63 (1964)

Brown-black ink on laid rice paper
Image: 22 × 10½; *paper:* 24 × 13

A sculpture called *Comet* by its owner was done the same
year (1964) as *Sunlit Straw* (see plate 62). This drawing
for *Comet* envisions it on a far more dramatic scale than
that of the completed piece, which is suspended (dramati-
cally enough) from the second-story ceiling of a private
home so as to reach almost all the way to the ground
floor.[33] Several years later, a somewhat similar piece that
does hang far overhead was created for a shopping center
in Flint, Michigan. The suggestion of overwhelming size
in this print is especially impressive. It is achieved entirely through the addition, and scale, of the human figures at the bottom of the plate. The appearance of airy
lightness here, as in the sculpture, is a result of the open
construction, a concept of modern metal sculpture that
Bertoia heartily endorsed. Both brown and black inks
were used in the graphic and, as with plate 62, there is
some evidence of afterimage from a previous print, although it is of little consequence to the completed
graphic.

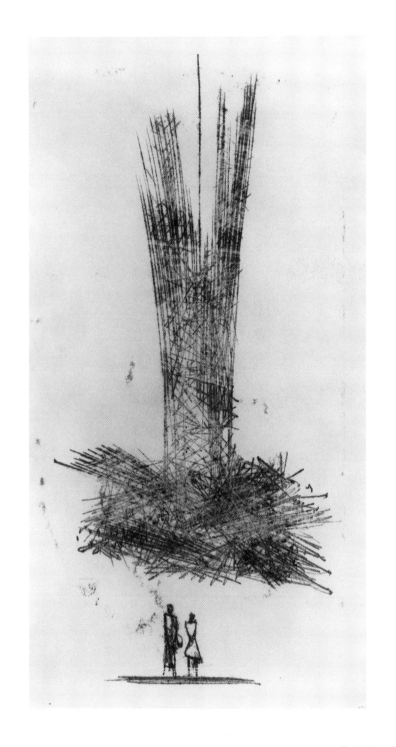

Plate 64 (late 1960s)

Blue and black ink on laid rice paper
Image: 18¼ × 37; paper: 24 × 39⅛

For this image from the late sixties, Bertoia returned to
the large paper size in a blue-ink drawing of great sureness, spontaneity, and grandeur. The image is of a single
sculptural form proceeding from two upright supports.
From the detail at the base of the stems and the linear
repetitions throughout, it is clear that this represents the
sculptural technique, which Bertoia used beginning about
1966, of bronze-welding copper rods side by side until
their juxtaposition and adhesion forms a metal plane. The
plane is not a smooth, single sheet of matter but rather a
skinlike membrane formed by the joining of many identical elements thereby giving an impression of elasticity.
Spaces are created on both sides of the plane.

In the print, the membrane of lines sweeps upward,
spreading outward in a continuous motion that curves
back and around to create loops and hollows, darks and
lights, negatives and positives. The result is an image as
of a gigantic contorted double mushroom or flower
growth. Its density, darkness, and apparent flexibility are
quite the opposite of the airiness, lightness, and rigidity
of the cages and straight-line constructions—and yet they
are related in their linearity. The ground line and areas of
granular shading were added in black ink, probably from
a second plate. (No plate marks of any kind are visible.)

This graphic may have established the groundwork for
fountain sculptures completed in Philadelphia and Buffalo in 1967 and 1968.[34] While the idea of two supports
for a single piece had been used before, it was not
adopted for either of these fountains.[35] However, its
gracefulness was never so successfully demonstrated as in
this drawing, whose image is one of baroque voluptuous-
ness in abstract form.

Plate 65 (late 1960s)

Black ink on laid rice paper
Image: 12¾ × 4⅜; *paper:* 19½ × 12⅛

A further development on paper—one that combines straight-line rigidity with curvaceous flexibility—is seen in this work, one of many black-ink prints depicting a standing square or rectangular box containing within it curved planes formed as described in the discussion of plate 64. If a sculpture exists based on these graphics, its present owner and location are not now known, but the intention to construct such a piece is clearly attested here. The drawings are an obvious attempt to carry further Bertoia's long-standing ideas concerning interior spaces of quiet refuge and the interpenetration of space.[36]

In the print, a membrane formed of repeated lines spans two rigid standing rectangular frames curving around to almost enclose dark interior spaces, which are the negative aspects of the outer (positive) surfaces of the membrane. It would appear from this drawing that the rectangular frame is open and that the lines forming the membrane emanate from its outer limits, the framework. The cavelike shapes of the interior are visible from both broad sides of the rectangle. While revealing the proposed structure, the drawing also achieves a sense of the tautness as well as the flexibility (in its malleable state) of the copper rod membrane that would form the sculpture.

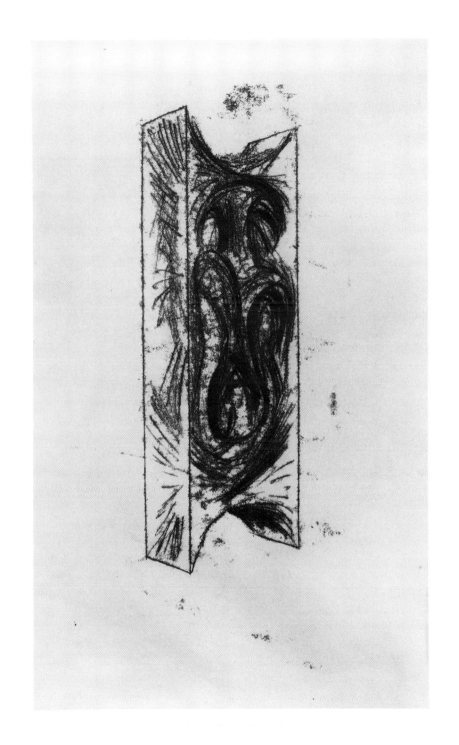

The 1970s

Clearly predominating in the graphics of Bertoia's last years are works related to his musical program. This is not surprising, in view of his preoccupation since the mid-sixties, almost to the point of obsession, with the sounding sculptures. Many of the related graphics of the seventies, however, explore forms for new booming or chiming sounds to accompany the standing flexible rods rather than new arrangements of the vertical sounding pieces themselves. Four of the five music-related drawings shown here are concerned with gongs—their shapes (sometimes playfully adapted to decorative compositions as in plates 77 and 78) and methods of supporting them. The other, plate 76, concerns itself with the form and disposition of the suspended metal rods dubbed "singing bars." Both gongs and singing bars were produced in metal and added to the grouping in the barn to increase the range and diversity of the *Sonambient* recordings.

As in the sixties, the paper works of the seventies display a continued emphasis on the sculptural. Except for plate 72, all those shown here tend to be form-oriented. Although many of the forms were not duplicated in metal, the images are a clear indication that Bertoia was thinking three-dimensionally. Cylinders and pipes and knotted filaments take on three-dimensional characteristics through compositional arrangements and the use of shading, cast shadows, and ground lines. Even the playful "frog" series (plates 66, 67, and 68), which starts out as a simple line drawing, evolves into a structure with sculptural possibilities.

While the seventies see the introduction of a number of new themes, there is, as always, an occasional renewal of old motifs. Plate 72, for example, refers back to the freehand linear repetitions of the 1940s, updating them into the elongated format and exploring a somewhat more subtle reversal of negative and positive. The knotted filaments of plate 71, which led to a group of small bronze-rod sculptures, are also reminiscent of the meandering repetitive lines of the forties, while the sweeping shaded curves of plate 79 bring to earth the rather more cosmic presentation of similar strokes used in California days.

The adaptation of cognates undergoes a reprise in the seventies after its virtual disappearance in the previous decade. The "frog" series and plate 70 attest its continued vitality in Bertoia's work. In the latter print especially, the softness of the background and the brown and black subtleties of the central area contrast effectively with the ghostly images, as well as with the strong positive ones.

Old interests in textures are also sometimes revived, as seen in plates 70, 72, 77, and 78. The textural effects achieved (and, one assumes, striven for), however, are not nearly as tactile as those of the block prints of the early forties. The effect is considerably more subtle now. The dramatic treatment of large forms with strong contrasts becomes more and more the norm as echoes of the granular backgrounds of the earliest works are seen only seldom.

The experimentation with new tools and materials, which had been a hallmark of Bertoia's monographics from the beginning but of which there is little evidence in the sixties because of his preoccupation with sculpture at that time, is revived in the seventies. The cylinders or rods used to draw plate 69 represent a new tool that expresses itself in sculptural terms, stroke and form being one. Experimentation with collage is seen in plate 78 and others like it. Such works are often frivolous or playful in nature. The use of stencils to print with, as in plate 77, is another tool not tried before the seventies. Its textural effects and image reversals are particularly interesting as they add a new twist to old concerns.

The tendency toward monochromatism in black ink continues. Again, it may have been a matter of expediency. As in the sixties, color, when added, is muted, and rarely are more than two colors used in a single work. Nevertheless, Bertoia's continued sensitivity to color is apparent in the black and brown striations of plate 70 and in other combinations of dark red, green, or blue with black, producing a variety of subtle gradations of tone.

The horizontal format continues to predominate, as does the use of laid rice paper. All monographics of the seventies reproduced here were printed on Bertoia's favorite paper, except plate 78, which, because it uses the collage technique, was done on much heavier paper. Its paper size, too, is different from that of all the others, each of which represents some torn dimension of the Sekishu paper that had come into standard use.[37] Only two of those shown here (plates 69 and 79) adopt the elongated dimension favored in the sixties which was half the height of a full sheet. All the others use a third of a sheet, torn top to bottom.[38]

Compositional elements in the graphics of the seventies continue the generally more curvate forms of the late sixties. Circles, cylinders, and other, more irregular, curves predominate. Only in the drawing for the singing bars (plate 76) and in the linear repetitions of plate 72 do we see anything like the geometric precision and straight-line rigidity of earlier decades, and even in these prints it is considerably modified.

In spite of their concentration on form, the monographics of the seventies consist largely of images that are non-representational. The early-twentieth-century rejection of realism in favor of the imagination remained a vital force in Bertoia's work right up to the end.

Plate 66 (1970s)

Black ink on laid rice paper
Image: 20½ × 7½; *paper:* 24⅞ × 13¼

This and the next two monographics make up a series illustrating the development of an idea in several stages. The first print is a simple line drawing transferred from a black inked plate. Circles are joined by pencil-thin curved lines to form a symmetrical standing figure of a whimsical nature. The succeeding graphics enlarge on this original theme, transforming it into completely new images each time.

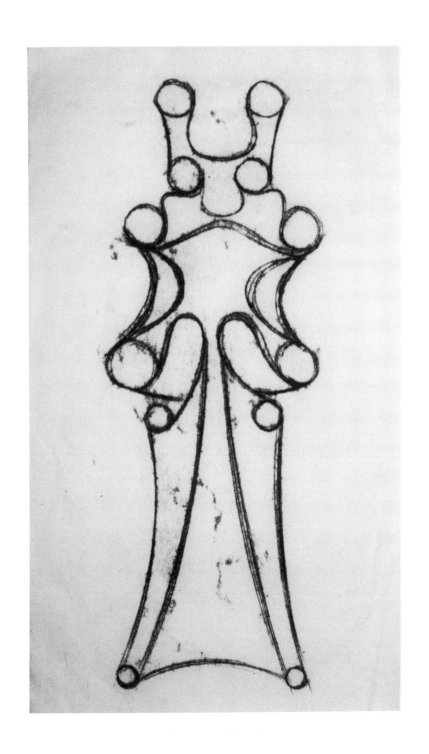

Plate 67 (1970s)

Black ink on laid rice paper
Image: 19⅞ × 7¼; *paper:* 24⅞ × 13¼

Using the same plate as the previous print, this, the second work in the series, has produced a somewhat similar yet different representation by drawing from the back of a new sheet of paper with the flat end of a balsa-wood stick. This method has resulted in strokes of varying thickness, each having a hard edge on the outside and a soft one on the inside. The strokes automatically give an effect of roundness to the form. Where the pressure of the wood stick crossed areas on the plate from which the ink had been removed by the earlier linear drawing, white lines appear on the new print.

The resulting figure has two bulging eyes at the top of its head, a pendulous snout, very short neck, and oval abdomen surrounded by short teddy-bear arms and legs bearing ball joints and terminals. This, the upper portion, rests on two long, outward-curving legs surrounded and joined by convex and concave curves as though in a webbing. As in the first print, the now fully three-dimensional image is seen in black ink against the white paper.

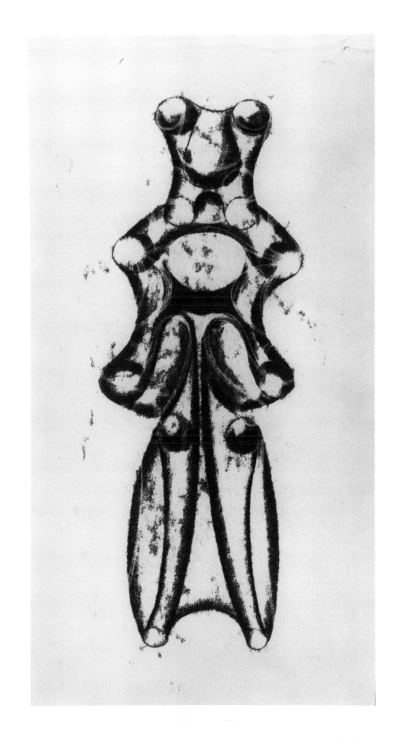

Plate 68 (1970s)

Black ink on laid rice paper
Image: 22⅝ × 9½; paper: 24⅞ × 13¼

The third print in the series that began with plate 66 shows an image appearing mostly white against a mottled-black background. Produced by brayer rubbing from behind, the broad background swath has picked up the negative not only of the image on plate 67 but also of the full extent of the earlier linear drawing of connected circles. A few truncated vestiges of the fine negative lines that are the afterimage of the original drawing can be seen in plate 67, but plate 68 contains the full ghost of both previous works. Many delicate black lines have been freely added to plate 68 in order to better define various parts of the new composition.

While the two prior prints both exhibited self-contained designs, plate 68, based as it is on negative images of the other two, presents a more complex composition of circular forms, a more stable structure, and a more convincing juncture of its upper and lower segments. It brings the series, each stage of which offers its own fully realized solution, to a satisfying completion.

Plate 69 (1970s)

Colored inks on laid rice paper
Image: 37 × 11; paper: 39 × 12

The image in this monographic was made using cylinders
as the drawing implements—probably cut and polished
sections of the beryllium copper rods Bertoia was using
for so much of his sculpture at the time. The plate was
first covered with a blend of green, brown, and black
inks. Rods or pipes of three different diameters were
used, first pressed on the back of the paper to make a circle, then dragged around in straight or curving fashion to
produce the cylinderlike design. The circles thus printed
appear lighter in the center, with firm outlines, and the
dragged areas connecting them take on the appearance
themselves of pipe cylinders. There are highlighted and
darkened areas in the long vertical composition that add
to the three-dimensional effect, all inked portions having
the granular texture so favored by Bertoia.

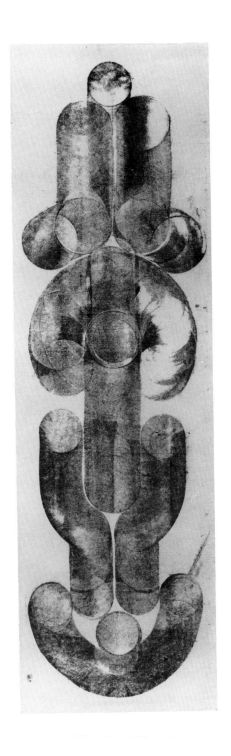

Plate 70 (1970s)

Black and brown ink on rice paper
Image: 22½ × 10⅞; paper: 24¾ × 12⅞

Rods or pipes used in Bertoia's sculpture were clearly the inspiration for plate 70. A double or divided pipe with two widely spaced swellings or undulations stands tall, hugging the left edge of the print. It was formed by three long, thick, vertical strokes using a beveled balsa-wood stick. A second similar representation appears just right of center, is somewhat more symmetrical, rests back farther on the ground plane, and is about four inches shorter than the first. Resting on the ground plane between the two tall figures is the image of a twisted rod lying on its rounded side with both cut ends indicated by sharp, straight lines. All three positive elements of the composition are drawn through a blend of black and brown inks, more black than brown.

Negative images overlap and flank the central group, the smaller ghosts having bulbous terminals while the large form, like its positive counterparts, is open-ended. The two smaller afterimages were produced by hand sweeps across the back of the paper and have granular backgrounds that are considerably more black than brown. The large one, however, is surrounded by light brown ink and was probably the result of pressure from a wire brush, to judge from the striations of brown and black ink. In several areas the negative images appear to overlay the positive, an indication that more than one plate may have been used.

The color variations and the softness of the ghostly negatives combine with the textural differentiations to create a monographic of unique and special beauty. In other versions of the same theme, the pipes float horizontally from end to end of the paper, suggesting blood vessels with their undulations and striations. Twisted rods like that seen here resting on the ground were produced as small sculptures but, so far as is known, no sculpture exists emulating the tall standing pipes of this series.

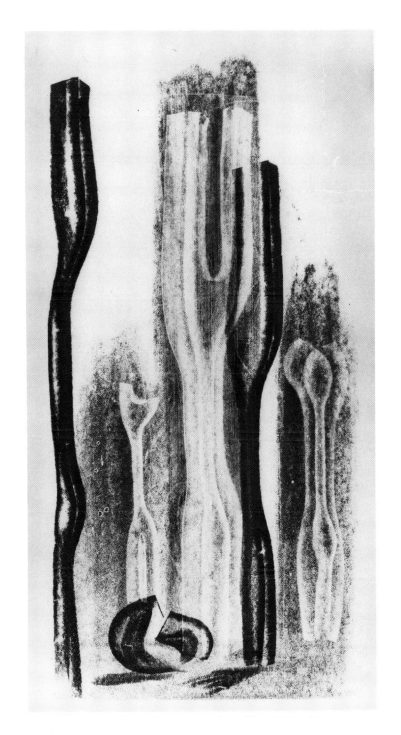

Plate 71 (1970s)

Red-black ink on rice paper
Images: each 4⅞ × 22⅞; *paper:* 13 × 24

Small sculptures exist of thin rods welded together to resemble the knotted linear forms of this monographic, which is an example of cognate prints on the same piece of paper. The plate used was quite short and wide and was inked all over with magenta and black. The lower of the two images was printed first and, except for a border of irregular intensity, has blank paper for background. On it are drawn three separate forms made up of many parallel lines which twist and turn into complex knotted shapes like braided filaments. Unlike the other two, the central form is not completely enclosed in its own knot but ends with its many lines streaming off to the right. At far left and here and there through the linear knots are negative traces of a previous drawing on the same plate.

On the upper half of the sheet is the afterimage of the full plate from which the lower drawing was printed. This can be plainly seen by turning the print upside down. The three large, knotted forms are now seen in negative along with the full but fainter residue of the earlier drawing mentioned above, completely reversing the highlights and shadows of the lower work. A few additional positive lines were added to the upper print, notably on either side of the central, large form and at the far left. The composition might have been improved by cutting off about three inches from the left side of each print. However, this would have necessitated splitting the paper in half to separate the two prints. As it stands, the tone reversal from lower to upper half intrigues, as it complements the intricacy of the knotted forms.

Plate 72 (1970s)

Blue-black and dark red ink on rice paper
Image: 11 × 22⅞; *paper:* 12¾ × 24

The use of repetitive line to produce form in his graphics
was a continuing interest of Bertoia's, which is under-
standable in view of his increasing use of rods and wires
for his sculptures. Plate 72 indicates that even when
sculptural form was not the object, the meandering repetition he had dealt with so often back in the forties retained a fascination for him. The lines, both negative and
positive, follow each other in undulating parallels across
the print, which resembles nothing so much as a wood
plank whose grain (including the knots) has been emphasized through staining. In several areas the repeated lines
cross each other forming a diamond grid reminiscent of
the metal-rod construction of the Bertoia chairs. The colors are dark blue at bottom shading into dark red at top.
Although the inking is consistent, it is possible that more
than one plate was used here, as there is a preponderance
of negative lines some of which extend beyond what appears to have been a plate edge or taped border at either
side.

Reminiscent of the forties also is the fact that this composition could be considered as either a horizontal or a
vertical one. In fact, when it is turned vertically, especially with the knots at the bottom, the change that
comes over the image is quite startling. Gone is the wood
grain effect, and instead of the peaceful sensation of
placid meanderings we receive a rush of exhilaration as
lines and forms seem to hurtle precipitously, almost diz-
zyingly, downward. (See also color plate.)

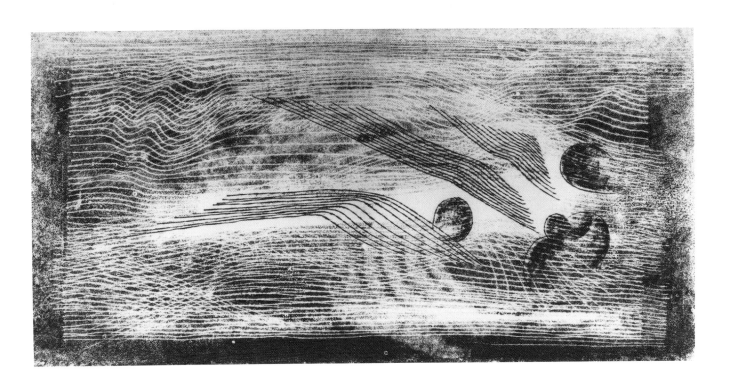

Plate 73 (1970s)

Brown-black ink on laid rice paper
Image: 10⅝ x 23⅛; *paper:* 13 × 25

Represented here on two levels in monochromatic
brown-black ink are a number of variations on a single
sculptural theme. None of the versions is unequivocally
identifiable with any known Bertoia sculpture but all of
them resemble to some degree the piece he did for the
Boyertown National Bank in Pennsylvania in 1974. Like
the larger, more voluptuous, fountain sculptures in Philadelphia and Buffalo, done in the late sixties, this work
was made of copper rods bronze-welded together side by
side to produce a sweeping curved membrane rising from
a growth-implying stem. The variations here represented
are drawn and shaded to reveal bud and flower shapes
that swell and curve, sometimes inward, sometimes outward, as they rise. The linearity of the juxtaposed rods is
summarily indicated in one or two of the drawings. Negative lines from a previous unrelated print invade some of
the drawn shapes, and ground lines or cast shadows are
indicated. As with music, so with the visual arts—variations on a single theme display the virtuosity of the
composer.

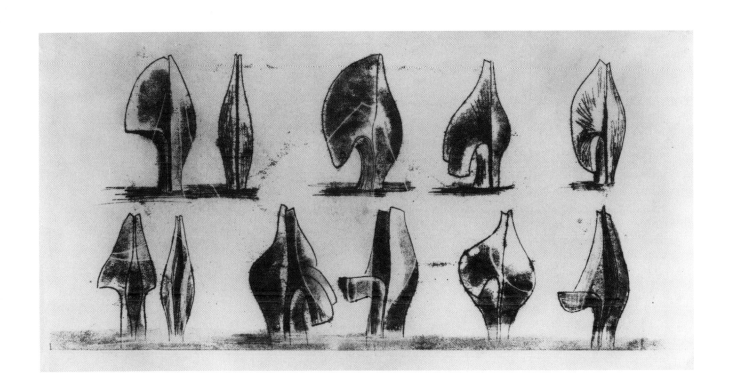

Plate 74 (1970s)

Black ink on laid rice paper
Image: 10 × 21; *paper:* 13 × 24

The sculptural image in plate 74 is of the twisted-rod variety seen in much smaller size in plate 70. Small sculptures such as this were produced by Bertoia in the seventies. Sometimes they were as simple as this, using a single twisted rod cut and polished so that the shiny circular ends contrasted with the dull matte surface of the twisted cylinder. Here the rod becomes impossibly gigantic by virtue of its domination of the entire picture space and by the addition of the relatively diminutive figure of a man in a business suit standing at right. Such a sculpture could never be made from a single piece of metal, but Bertoia may have dreamed of producing something so overwhelming through the use of other materials and methods. Or perhaps it was just another of his whimsical ideas. The form in this monochromatic print has been realized by shading alone, including the distinction between shiny and matte surfaces. The lines came later—or earlier in the case of the negative ones, which are from a prior print. In the flat circle at right, the impression of the fingers of the right hand can be seen to have started the stroke of granular ink which swept from bottom to top.[39]

Plate 75 (1970s)

Black ink on laid rice paper
Image: 11 × 22; *paper:* 13 × 24

In the course of the development of Bertoia's musical program, other sounds were sought in addition to those pro-
ducible by the flexible rods. Since in playing the instruments inside their sounding box (the barn), the performer
walked slowly around and among the sculptures, touching or rubbing as he went, a most logical accompaniment
—since it could also be played by touching or rubbing—
was a gong. And of course a number of different resonant
tones could be produced by varying the shapes, the thicknesses, and the alloys.

Many designs were made for gong shapes, which were
then suspended from the ceiling (see plates 59, 77, and
78), and, as this monographic indicates, a number of
ground-level supports were also tried. In this monochromatic drawing, the forms were realized by being drawn
with a stylus and shaded by hand pressure. The sizes and
angles of the gong heads represented combine with the
overlapping of some of the structures to give a sense of
balance to the graphic composition. A few works such as
these were produced, exhibited, and sold in the seventies
as sculptures for outdoor installation.

Plate 76 (1970s)

Black ink on laid rice paper
Image: 11 × 20½; *paper:* 13⅛ × 25¼

Another type of sculpture-instrument devised during the seventies as an adjunct to the *Sonambient* program consisted of two or more suspended rigid rods which, when touched, moved together to produce metallic tones. Represented in plate 76 are four different arrangements of the "singing bars," as they came to be called. Reading from right to left in the print (which would be left to right as drawn) are groupings as noted beneath each one of "2 sounds," "5 sounds," "2 bars equal length, one sound," and "3 sounds." The bars vary in length and are balanced sometimes horizontally; sometimes angled and close together, each on its own cord or wire; and in one instance attached angularly at different points along a single suspension. In their sculptural form, a touch sets them in motion and they produce intermittent sound as they move and clang together. The sounds emanating from them depend on the length and positioning of the rods as well as on the particular metal of which they are made. They are enriched visually by their own cast shadows, especially when in motion. The monochromatic black-ink print clearly and simply shows the visual aspects of balance and capability of motion that are inherent qualities of these sculptural pieces.

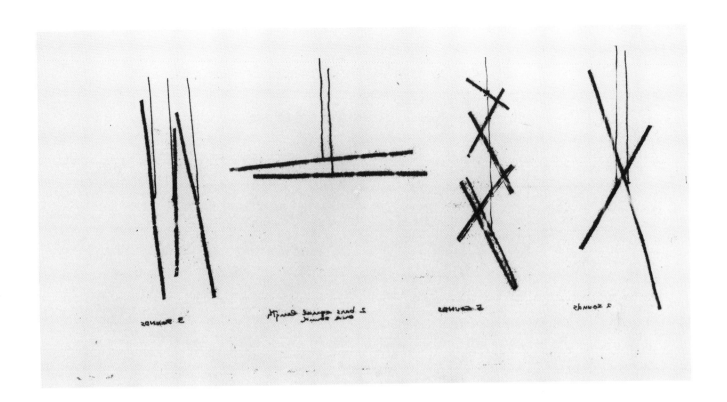

Plate 77 (1970s)

Black ink on rice paper
Image: 10⅞ × 23⅞; *paper:* 13⅛ × 24⅞

Two further works occasioned by the musical program
are plates 77 and 78. Both are representations of gong
shapes and both use stencils in different ways to produce
their images. The present plate is the more complex of
the two, at least in its process. It would appear that three
shapes were first cut out of a pebbly-textured paper. The
two large ones were inked on one surface and hand-
rubbed directly onto the already partially inked glass or
Masonite plate, the larger of the two overlapping the
third, small, round shape, which had been laid, uninked,
on the plate. The cutouts were then picked up, reversed,
and laid down again on the plate, inked-side up, overlapping their own previously made images. The paper was
laid over the plate, and an impression made of the whole.
At this time the earlier forms were outlined and the word
"sounds" was written at the lower right (it can barely be
seen in reverse through the dark smudge at lower left in
the photo). The white line around the second use of the
forms must have been scratched around them as they lay
on the plate prior to printing.

This intricate juggling of cutout shapes has produced
yet another intriguing print in which dark and light, negative and positive are playfully juxtaposed. The forms—
circles and rounded squares with indentations and "eye"
openings—are those conceived for, and made into, suspended metal gongs that accompany the *Sonambient*
reeds.

Plate 78 (1970s)

Colored inks and collage on heavy rice paper
Image: 22½ × 18½; paper: 26⅜ × 20½

Here, in a collage, gong shapes similar to those used in
the last plate were cut out of paper and inked, this time
blue-green. Probably they were used for printing another
work, after which Bertoia found their inked surfaces appealing and decided to adapt them. They were pasted on
heavy paper, and strong, directional, dark brown lines
from a felt-tipped pen were drawn with great vigor across
their surfaces and the paper. The three forms are unconnected with each other and present a somehow amusing
appearance as they float across the blank, white space
with their linear accompaniments. The holes and indentations of the three forms were Bertoia's solution to the
practical problem of hanging the gongs.

Plate 79 (1978)

Black ink on laid rice paper
Image: 11 × 37½; *paper:* 12 × 39

The musical program was Bertoia's major preoccupation of the 1970s. Most of the commissions of those years were realized in terms of sounding sculptures, including his largest, for the Standard Oil Plaza in Chicago, completed in 1975, and his last, for the Federal Reserve Bank of Richmond, completed in July 1978. Throughout the years of constructing large works which then had to be crated and shipped elsewhere, he often spoke somewhat wistfully of doing a gigantic piece somewhere on his own land where, once finished, it would remain. Among his last printed drawings, plate 79 is one of several that recorded ideas for this proposed undertaking, unfortunately never realized.

For this monochromatic print, repeated undulating lines were drawn so that each broad line has an outer sharp edge that shades off to nothing on the inside, the same technique as that used in plates 67 and 70. Each stroke more or less repeats the last in gradually increasing height and length until the final stroke sweeps from side to side of the elongated page, swelling just left of center in a manner that resembles a hill or mound of earth. The undulating hills protectively surround an off-center motif of an irregularly curved form, itself made up of four similar repetitive strokes around a tall opening. This form is shaped somewhat like other drawings of the seventies that explore in sculptural terms the motif of an aeolian harp as a giant-size, stringed instrument set up out of doors to be played by the winds. Here, it has more the appearance of a gateway with horizontal strokes across the ground in the opening to indicate recession in depth. The idea of an outdoor setting is completed by the granular ground containing short vertical lines of growth.

Apart from its representational inclinations, this, one of Bertoia's last graphic works, bears a close affinity, in its repeated shadowy curves rising from the ground, to works such as plate 22 done in 1944. It affords proof of the validity of a long-standing idea and is a final demonstration of the interrelationship between Bertoia's sculptures and his monographics.

6. Chronology

Note: Exhibitions are one-man sculpture exhibitions unless otherwise indicated.

Year	Events	Sculpture Commissions	Exhibitions
1915	*March 10:* born at San Lorenzo, Udine, Italy		
1928	First art lessons (drawing)		
1930	To Canada and then Detroit with his father		
1936	Graduates Cass Technical High School, Detroit, Michigan		
1936	Scholarship to School of the Detroit Society of Arts and Crafts		
1937	Teaching scholarship to Cranbrook Academy of Art, Bloomfield Hills, Michigan, where he teaches metalworking until 1942; graphics, 1942–43		
1938	First forays in print shop at Cranbrook		
1940	Meets Brigitta Valentiner, a student at Cranbrook		
1943	*May 10:* marries Brigitta Valentiner. *October:* moves to Los Angeles to work with Charles Eames; settles in small beach house near Malibu		*Summer:* 19 "monoprints" at the Museum of Non-objective Painting, New York. *Fall:* monotypes and jewelry at Cranbrook Academy of Art; monotypes and jewelry at Nierendorf Gallery, New York
1944	Studies welding at Santa Monica City College; birth of daughter, Mara Lesta; meets Oskar Fischinger		
1945			Monotypes at San Francisco Museum of Art
1945–47	Stipend from Nierendorf		
1946	Breaks with Eames; moves to Topanga Canyon		
1947	*October:* Receives U.S. citizenship; begins welding sculpture; Karl Nierendorf dies		Last show of monotypes and jewelry at Nierendorf Gallery

Year	Events	Sculpture Commissions	Exhibitions
1947–49	Graphic work at Point Loma Naval Electronics Laboratory; moves to La Jolla		
1949	Birth of son, Val Odey		
1950	*Summer:* moves to New Hope, Pennsylvania to design for Knoll Associates		
1951	Works on chair design		Knoll Associates, New York
1952	Leases, then buys, farm in Barto, Pennsylvania; voted Visiting Critic in Sculpture, Yale University, for 1953–54 at request of Josef Albers. *December:* Bertoia chair introduced by Knoll		*December:* chair, sculptures, and "monoprints" at Knoll Associates, New York
1953	*Fall:* working relationship with Knoll terminates; continues to consult; acquires studio in Bally, Pennsylvania	First architectural sculpture commission: General Motors Technical Center, Warren, Michigan—sculpture screen	
1953–54			Sculpture on loan to Museum of Modern Art, New York
1954		Manufacturers Hanover Trust Co., New York—screen and hanging sculpture; Cincinnati Public Library—sculpture screen	Sculptures and monotypes at Massachusetts Institute of Technology
1955	Birth of daughter, Celia Marei. *July:* reads paper and shows "Graphic Poem" slides at International Design Conference, Aspen, Colorado; awarded gold medal of the Architectural League of New York. *October:* Hans Knoll dies	Massachusetts Institute of Technology Chapel—reredos; Dallas Public Library—sculpture screen; Lambert Airport, St. Louis—sculpture screen	
1956	Awarded gold medal of the Architectural League of New York; awarded Craftsmanship Medal by American Institute of Architects	Dayton Store, Edina, Minnesota—2 screens; U.S. Consulates, Bremen and Düsseldorf—gong sculptures	*December 3–29:* first one-man exhibition at Fairweather Hardin Gallery, Chicago; represented, Museum of Contemporary Crafts, New York
1956–57			Smithsonian Institution traveling exhibition, one-man show of sculptures, monotypes, furniture (10 museums)

Year	Events	Sculpture Commissions	Exhibitions
1957	Awarded $10,000 fellowship by Graham Foundation for Advanced Studies in the Fine Arts. *Spring:* first trip to Italy since emigrating; awarded Craftsmanship Medal by American Institute of Design	First National Bank, Tulsa, Oklahoma—fountain sculpture; U.S. Pavilion, Brussels World's Fair—tree sculpture	Cranbrook Academy of Art Museum; represented, American exhibition, Art Institute of Chicago; represented, "Forged in Fire," American Federation of Arts traveling exhibition
1958	*September:* William Valentiner dies	Yale University—gilded screen	Galeria Don Hatch, Caracas, Venezuela; represented, "Living Today," Corcoran Gallery of Art; represented, "Sculpture 1950–1958," Allen Memorial Art Museum, Oberlin College; represented, Carnegie International
1959	Citation for furniture design, Philadelphia Museum College of Art	First National Bank, Miami—10 screens; Zenith Radio Corp., Chicago—wall-hung sculpture	Represented, "Recent Sculpture, USA," Museum of Modern Art traveling exhibition; Virginia Museum of Fine Arts, Richmond
1960	Produces first standing sounding sculptures		Represented, American Sculptors exhibition, Galerie Claude Bernard, Paris
1961	Tamarind Lithography Workshop fellowship offered and refused. *June:* Visit to Ossabaw Island; Eero Saarinen dies	Denver Hilton Hotel—screen and wire sphere on stem; St. John's Unitarian Church, Cincinnati—wall-hung sculpture; Albright-Knox Art Gallery, Buffalo—sculpture screen; Eastman Kodak Co., Rochester, New York—wall-hung sculpture	Fairweather Hardin Gallery, Chicago; first show of sculpture at Staempfli Gallery, New York; Museum of Modern Art, Buenos Aires, under Knoll auspices; represented, "Drawings USA," St. Paul Art Center, Minnesota
1962		Syracuse University—ceiling sculpture; Bankers Trust Co., New York—wall-hung sculpture; Dulles International Airport, Chantilly, Virginia—poured-bronze screen	
1963	Awarded Fine Arts Medal by the Pennsylvania Association of the American Institute of Architects; Mrs. Valentiner dies	Perpetual Savings & Loan Association, Los Angeles—fountain sculpture (now at Joslyn Art Museum, Omaha)	Staempfli Gallery, New York; European traveling exhibition under Knoll auspices—sculpture and graphics

Year	Events	Sculpture Commissions	Exhibitions
1964	Film, *Harry Bertoia's Sculpture*, made by Clifford West	Eastman Kodak Pavilion, New York World's Fair—wire "dandelions"; W. Hawkins Ferry, Grosse Pointe Shores, Michigan—*Comet*; Golden West Savings Association, Castro Valley, California—ceiling sculpture; Princeton University—globe sculpture; Northwestern National Life Insurance Co., Minneapolis—*Sunlit Straw*	
1965	Travels to Spain	Cuyahoga Savings Association, Cleveland, Ohio—hanging sculpture; Southwestern Bell, Houston, Texas—hanging sphere	
1966	Travels to Belgium and the Netherlands	River Oaks Shopping Center, Calumet City, Illinois—fountain sculpture	Knoll showrooms in Belgium and the Netherlands; represented, "Drawings USA," St. Paul Art Center, Minnesota
1967	Travels to Zurich; award for excellence in sculpture, Philadelphia Arts Festival	Federal Court Building, Brooklyn, New York—sculpture screen; Philadelphia Civic Center—fountain; Whiting Auditorium, Flint, Michigan—hanging sphere	Knoll showroom in Zurich, Switzerland
1968	Designs Architecture Critic's Medal for American Institute of Architects	Rochester Institute of Technology—3 poured-bronze cubes; Manufacturers and Traders Trust Co., Buffalo—fountain	Fairweather Hardin Gallery, Chicago; Staempfli Gallery, New York; represented, "Drawings USA," St. Paul Art Center, Minnesota
1968–69	Barn at Barto is remodeled to hold sounding sculptures		
1970	First *Sonambient* recordings	Genessee Valley Shopping Center, Flint, Michigan—hanging sculpture	Staempfli Gallery, New York
1971	Honorary Doctor of Fine Arts, Muhlenberg College, Allentown, Pennsylvania; film, *Sonambients: The Sound Sculpture of Harry Bertoia*, made by Jeffrey Eger	Lake Clifton Senior High School, Baltimore, Maryland—copper-tube sculpture	
1972	Travels to Oslo; *Sonambient* registered as trademark. *December*: Brother Oreste dies	Marshall University, Huntington, West Virginia—fountain sculpture	Gallery KB, Oslo, Norway; Staempfli Gallery, New York

Year	Events	Sculpture Commissions	Exhibitions
1973	Awarded Fine Arts medal by American Institute of Architects at national convention, San Francisco		Marshall University, Huntington, West Virginia—sculpture and graphics; Court Gallery, Copenhagen; Mitchell Art Museum, Mt. Vernon, Illinois; represented (11 works), "Sound Sculpture," Vancouver Art Gallery
1974	Travels to Alberta, Canada, for Christmas to visit his mother and sister	Edith Abbott Memorial Library, Grand Island, Nebraska—steel sculpture; National Bank of Boyertown, Pennsylvania—fountain; A. Price Woodard Memorial, Wichita, Kansas—copper-rod sculpture	Wadsworth Atheneum, Lions Gallery of the Senses, Hartford, Connecticut—sounding sculptures
1975	Eastman Kodak Company gives 7 gilded "dandelions" of 1964 to Rochester Institute of Technology	Standard Oil Plaza, Chicago, Illinois—11 sounding sculptures; Music, Speech and Theatre Arts Building, University of Akron, Ohio—5 sounding sculptures; Annenberg Center, University of Pennsylvania, Philadelphia—hanging sculpture; Swann Oil Company, Bala-Cynwyd, Pennsylvania—*Energizing*, standing screen	Gallery KB, Oslo, Norway. *April:* Fairweather Hardin Gallery, Chicago; Art Institute of Chicago
1975–76			*December–February:* Allentown Art Museum, sculpture and graphics
1976	*January:* travels to Cuzco, Machu Picchu, Lima, Yucatan, Guatemala, and Mexico City; Honorary Doctor of Humane Letters, Lehigh University, Bethlehem, Pennsylvania. *May:* Travels with Brigitta to Bergen and Oslo, Norway	Colorado National Bank, Denver—sounding sculpture; Allentown-Bethlehem-Easton Airport—hanging sculpture; U.S. Embassy, Oslo—gong sculpture; Sun Oil Company Headquarters, Radnor, Pennsylvania—suspended sculpture; Alumni Center, Bowling Green State University, Ohio—sounding sculpture	National Academy of Arts and Sciences, Washington, D.C.; Grieg Hall, Bergen, Norway; Gallery KB, Oslo, Norway; Staempfli Gallery, New York
1977	*March:* travels to Caracas, speaks to architecture students of University of Venezuela. *Fall:* persistent laryngitis lasting until March 1978	Sentry Insurance Company World Headquarters, Stevens Point, Wisconsin—sculpture screen of rods	Galeria Hatch, Caracas, Venezuela; Joslyn Art Museum, Omaha; Marshall University, Huntington, West Virginia—sculpture and graphics

Year	Events	Sculpture Commissions	Exhibitions
1978	*January:* travels to Bahamas for his health. *May:* travels to Oslo and Bergen. *June:* travels to Colorado to visit his daughter, Celia. *September:* fire in Heinie-Onstad Museum storeroom destroys 2 sculptures and 12 graphics. *September–October:* travels to California and Mexico for treatment. *November 6:* dies at his home in Barto, Pennsylvania	Federal Reserve Bank, Richmond, Virginia—double sounding sculpture	Hokin Gallery, Palm Beach, Florida; Gallery KB, Oslo; Grieg Hall, Bergen; and Heinie-Onstad Museum, Høvikodden, Norway—sculpture and graphics. *October 17–November 11:* Staempfli Gallery, New York. *October 22–November 19:* Carl Schlosberg Fine Arts, Sherman Oaks, California
1979			Fairweather Hardin Gallery, Chicago; Benjamin Mangel Gallery, Bala-Cynwyd, Pennsylvania
1980	First Hazlett Memorial Award for excellence in the arts in Pennsylvania; posthumous publication of *Fifty Drawings*		Cranbrook Academy of Art Museum
1981			Staempfli Gallery, New York—retrospective; Wyomissing Institute of Fine Arts
1983			Benjamin Mangel Gallery, Philadelphia
1984			Fairweather Hardin Gallery, Chicago—monographics

Notes

1. Introduction

1. For Bertoia's sculpture prior to 1970, see June Kompass Nelson, *Harry Bertoia, Sculptor*.

2. "Chemically Pure in Art."

3. Allen, *Tamarind*, 8.

4. Johnson, *American Prints*, 71.

5. Brooklyn Museum, *American Artist*, 11.

6. June Wayne to Harry Bertoia, August 24 and August 29, 1961 and October 23, 1964. Bertoia files, Val Bertoia, Barto, Pennsylvania.

7. Hayter, *About Prints*, 103–4.

8. Johnson, *American Prints*, 17.

9. Mary Jane Jacob, "The Modern Art Gallery 1932–1941," in (Detroit Institute of Arts) *Arts and Crafts*, 168.

10. Ibid.

11. Lukach, *Hilla Rebay*, 141.

12. Ibid., 146.

13. The invited contributors included Thomas Hart Benton, Peter Blume, Charles Burchfield, John Steuart Curry, Edward Hopper, Peter Hurd, Yasuo Kuniyoshi, Reginald Marsh, Charles Sheeler, John Sloan, Raphael Soyer, and Grant Wood, to name the best known (Cranbrook Academy, *Cranbrook-"Life" Exhibition*). A letter also exists in the Cranbrook Archives, dated February 6, 1940, from Margit Varga of *Life* to Richard P. Raseman, executive secretary of Cranbrook Academy of Art, enclosing a list of seventy artists from whom the fifty were chosen.

14. A loan exhibition from the Solomon R. Guggenheim Foundation. Lukach, *Hilla Rebay*, 146. Confirmed by telephone conversation with Lydia Winston Malbin, January 3, 1987.

15. Lukach, *Hilla Rebay*, 147.

16. Rosenblum, *Cubism*, 222.

17. The quote from Thomas Messer is in Lukach, *Hilla Rebay*, 309.

18. Seitz, *Abstract Expressionist Painting*, 151.

19. Allen, *Tamarind*, 8.

20. Castleman, *Prints*, 129.

21. From May through July of 1943 (Lukach, *Hilla Rebay*, 155).

22. Dated 18 June 1943. Ibid., 149.

23. (Metropolitan Museum) *Painterly Print*, ix.

24. Between the time this was originally written and the date of publication, four of the monographics were sold.

25. The *Oxford Dictionary of the English Language* gives first usage in 1880. However, *Webster's Ninth New Collegiate Dictionary* gives 1882.

26. Rasmusen, *Printmaking with Monotype*, 15. Rasmusen cites three methods, but the third is essentially a combination of the first two.

27. Michael Mazur, "Monotype: An Artist's View," in (Metropolitan Museum) *Painterly Print*, 57.

28. Eugenia Parry Janis, "Setting the Tone—The Revival of Etching, the Importance of Ink," in (Metropolitan Museum) *Painterly Print*, 27.

29. The *Oxford Dictionary of the English Language* and the *American Heritage Dictionary* continue to ignore the word completely.

30. See Michael Mazur's distinction in "Monotype," in (Metropolitan Museum) *Painterly Print*, 62.

31. Rasmusen, *Printmaking with Monotype*, 3. The italics are Rasmusen's.

32. Ibid., 4.

33. Ibid., 47.

34. Colta Ives, "The Modern Art of Monotype," in (Metropolitan Museum) *Painterly Print*, 51.

35. Ivins, *How Prints Look*, 146.

36. The author acknowledges with grateful thanks the cooperation of Brigitta Bertoia, widow of the artist, who spent many hours going over the circumstances surrounding the production of each of the monographics in order to determine as closely as possible the year or the decade in which each was produced. Mrs. Bertoia's recollections were of invaluable assistance on this project.

37. Two were published in 1970. See Nelson, *Harry Bertoia, Sculptor*, pls. 11 and 13.

38. University of Louisville, Kentucky, 1953; Massachusetts Institute of Technology, 1954; University of California, Davis, 1955; Oshkosh Public Museum, Wisconsin, 1956; and Nebraska State Teachers College, Chadron, 1958; among others. Registrar's office, card index file, Solomon R. Guggenheim Museum, New York.

39. See Nelson, *Harry Bertoia, Sculptor*, pl. 12.

2. Biography

1. Quoted by Cass, "Musician's Sculptor."

2. Dino de Paoli to Brigitta Bertoia, December 1979, (possession of recipient). Dino de Paoli, of Alberta, Canada, Harry's nephew, transcribed the story from a conversation in Italian with Harry's mother, Maria Bertoia, and sister, Ave de Paoli.

3. Mary Louise Davis (retired 1950) and Louise Larned Green (retired 1946) were both brought to Cass Tech through the efforts of Albert Kahn, the architect. Lydia Winston Malbin, telephone conversation (see chap. 1, n. 14); Malbin is the daughter of Albert Kahn. The quotations are from Bertoia, conversation with Fairweather and Hoff, tape 1, side A. (I am indebted to Sally Fairweather for the opportunity to listen to these tapes.)

4. The painting is owned by Bertoia's sister, Ave de Paoli, Alberta, Canada.

5. Bertoia, conversation with Fairweather and Hoff, tape 1, side A.

6. Richard Raseman, executive secretary of Cranbrook Academy, wrote, "Harry Bertoia, Instructor of Metal Work, is a young man of great possibilities. It is to be regretted that the days are not twice as long, as he is also an accomplished painter and wood engraver. He can use all the encouragement the Academy can give him." (Cranbrook Academy of Art semi-annual report, January 23, 1940, Cranbrook Archives, Records of the Cranbrook Foundation Trustees, Series 1, Box 3, Cranbrook Academy of Art, Annual Reports 1933–1942). The reference to wood engraving may have alluded to some woodcuts Bertoia did early in his experimentation in the print shop.

7. Quoted by Robert Judson Clark, "Cranbrook and the Search for Twentieth Century Form," in (Detroit Institute of Arts) *Design in America*, 29–30.

8. Bertoia, conversation with Fairweather and Hoff, tape 2, side A.

9. Clark, "Cranbrook," in (Detroit Institute of Arts) *Design in America*, 31.

10. Bertoia, conversation with Fairweather and Hoff, tape 2, side A.

11. After leaving school to go their various ways, the Cranbrook alumniae tended to continue to call upon each other as consultants and specialists in different fields. For instance, Charles Eames's use of Bertoia and others in the designing of the so-called Eames chair; Florence and Hans Knoll's signing on of both Eero Saarinen and Bertoia as furniture designers; Eero Saarinen's several commissions for Bertoia sculptures to enhance his buildings.

12. However, at the time of his first real success in 1943, Bertoia was twenty-eight years old. As a result of emigration from Italy at age fifteen and a consequent language difficulty, he had not graduated from high school until he was twenty-one.

13. Burrows, "Review." The implication, in this review, of general disapproval of the geometric nature of many nonobjective works is typical of the reception they were getting from critics and public as late as 1943.

14. The gallery contact may have been additionally stimulated by Dr. Valentiner who had known Karl Nierendorf for some time.

15. Bertoia's status in the United States in 1943 was that of an enemy alien. His offer to join the U.S. Army had been refused.

16. In an interview with the author at Bally on August 24, 1966, Bertoia said, "I was instrumental in contributing some form to the Eames chair." Among others who contributed, he said, were Gregory Ayn and Herbert Matter. In a later interview at Bally, January 8, 1967, Bertoia said with regard to the dispute over the Eames chair, "No purpose would be served by making a big issue of it now. However, it *did* happen and there is no reason not to record it as a matter of fact." Bertoia did pursue the matter after an article appeared in *Fortune* in 1949, as letters from C. D. Jackson, publisher of *Fortune* (August 31), George Nelson (September 8), and Charles Eames (September 9) attest (Bertoia files, Val Bertoia, Barto, Pennsylvania). Clifford West (in a telephone conversation with the author, January 3, 1985) confirms that Bertoia was responsible for the invention of the metalwork on the Eames chair. For a full recounting by Bertoia, see McGhee, "Influences," 98–105.

17. Ray Eames (in a telephone conversation with the author, January 17, 1985) stated that while most of the crew worked nights as well as days on the chair, Bertoia was never asked to give up his evenings at home.

18. Nierendorf Gallery exhibition review (1945), 25.

19. Bertoia, "Five Drawings."

20. Both her mother's "Graphic Poem" and the group of sixty-seven drawings are still in the possession of Brigitta Bertoia.

21. Three of the drawings in this series were among those reproduced in *Arts and Architecture* in 1945 from the "book of eighty-four."

22. Harry Bertoia to Kaare Berntsen, April 14, 1977. Bertoia files, Val Bertoia, Barto, Pennsylvania.

23. Harry Bertoia to Kaare Berntsen, September 18, 1978. A photostatic copy of this letter in Bertoia's handwriting is in his Kaare Berntsen file, Bertoia files, Val Bertoia, Barto, Pennsylvania.

24. See Nelson, *Harry Bertoia, Sculptor*, pl. 19.

25. Hans Knoll's original idea was for him to design a suite of furniture suitable for hospitals (Willenbecher, "Harry Bertoia"). During the design process, somehow the original idea became lost.

26. The other pieces include a large diamond chair, a high-backed chair with ottoman, a side chair, and two children's chairs (see Nelson, *Harry Bertoia, Sculptor*, pl. 18.

27. For a sampling of these, see ibid., pl. 20.

28. Ibid., pl. 21.

29. Many Knoll showroom managers acted as unofficial agents for Bertoia's sculptures with their clients.

30. "Verbal inadequacy on my part, results from a strong desire to observe in silence, then generate" (Bertoia, "Light and Structure").

31. The date of 1963, given for the completion of this commission in my earlier book, is incorrect.

32. During the late sixties, in fact, Bertoia found it frequently necessary to refuse commissions he knew he would be unable to complete on time.

33. This was one of several invitational exhibitions Bertoia entered. However, there were many others he had to refuse.

34. Knoll Associates exhibition review.

35. West, *Harry Bertoia's Sculpture*.

36. More beryllium copper was ordered in 1967, and in 1969 Bertoia took advantage of a special offer from his supplier to order over five-thousand pounds. Apparently he ignored the warning label attached to a letter received from the supplier at the time of his first large order, which read, "*WARNING.* Do not breathe dust or fumes generated by mechanical, thermal or chemical processing." His ne-

glect of wearing a mask while welding was the probable cause of his death more than ten years later.

37. A task he took on somewhat reluctantly. Although he handled English fairly well, he continued to be shy about public speaking in the language.

38. Brigitta Bertoia retains a cast-gold gong-shaped pendant, one of the few relics of this project.

39. Shops managed by the wives of Harry Weese in Chicago and Ralph Rapson in Boston (Harry Weese to Harry Bertoia, n.d. [ca. 1948], Ralph Rapson to Harry Bertoia, October 13 and November 9, 1949, Bertoia files, Val Bertoia, Barto, Pennsylvania).

40. Renée S. Nau, assistant curator, Museum of Modern Art to Harry Bertoia, October 25, 1966 (Bertoia files, Val Bertoia, Barto, Pennsylvania). Bertoia's handwritten comments at bottom include, "No idea where to find any of the jewelry done. We have kept none."

41. To Harry's great sorrow, Oreste died in December 1972. For a picture of Bertoia "playing" some of the sculptures, see Nelson, *Harry Bertoia, Sculptor*, pl. 72. At this writing, the sculptures are still in the barn at Barto.

42. Harry Bertoia to Norman Lloyd, July 7, 1971 (unsigned, possibly unfinished, letter in Bertoia's handwriting, addressed to the Rockefeller Foundation), *Sonambient* file, Bertoia files, Barto, Pennsylvania.

43. Registration no. 939,885. Richard O. Church to Harry Bertoia, August 23, 1972, *Sonambient* file, Bertoia files, Val Bertoia, Barto, Pennsylvania. As early as 1968, Bertoia had looked into the possibility of patenting his sound sculptures but apparently gave it up when advised that a patent would provide little useful protection. The registered trademark covered the term *Sonambient* as used to indicate a grouping of the sculptures to provide a new kind of tonal music. Bertoia's interest in patents and trademarks no doubt stemmed from his experience with Eames and his seeing in 1962 a *Life* photograph of a fountain in Australia based on a design proposal he had given to an Australian architect whom he never heard from again.

44. Some of the titles of the later recorded performances are "Ocean Mysteries," "Softly Played," "Here and Now," and "Unknown."

45. Filmed by Jeffrey Eger.

46. Quoted in Artner, "Sounding Out."

47. Sally Huyser to Harry Bertoia, November 18, 1977. Bertoia files, Val Bertoia, Barto, Pennsylvania.

48. "Your letter has just come and all of us at Fairweather Hardin are celebrating the wonderful news you have given us. . . . It sounds as if you got to Dr. Norris in plenty of time, which means that you and we and the rest of humanity can look forward to countless more Bertoias!" (Sally Fairweather to Harry Bertoia, March 29, 1978). Bertoia files, Val Bertoia, Barto, Pennsylvania.

49. His last one-man exhibition opened at Staempfli Gallery in New York on October 17 and ran until November 11, five days after his death.

50. Harry Bertoia to Kaare Berntsen, September 18, 1978 (Kaare Berntsen file, Bertoia files, Val Bertoia, Barto, Pennsylvania).

51. Harry Bertoia to Kaare Berntsen, October 20, 1978 (Bertoia files, Val Bertoia, Barto, Pennsylvania). The original in Bertoia's handwriting on two sheets of ruled paper is in his Kaare Berntsen file. He was in the habit of writing letters out in longhand to establish what he wanted to say. If it satisfied him, he had it photostated to keep a copy for his file and sent the original. Otherwise, he rewrote it with changes and kept the original. This letter has no scribbled changes but was probably rewritten, because the original is on scrap paper.

52. Harry Bertoia to Kaare Berntsen, copy of Western Union mailgram, October 23, 1978, Kaare Berntsen file, Bertoia files, Val Bertoia, Barto, Pennsylvania.

53. According to the death certificate (Harry Bertoia scrapbook, Brigitta Bertoia, Barto, Pennsylvania).

54. Ibid.

3. Tools and Techniques

1. Quoted in McGhee, "Influences," 88.

2. Ibid.

3. Bertoia, *Fifty Drawings*.

4. Bertoia, conversation with Fairweather and Hoff, tape 1, side B.

5. Cass, "Musician's Sculptor."

6. For a discussion of Gauguin's works, see Barbara Stern Shapiro, "Nineteenth Century Masters of the Painterly Print," in (Metropolitan Museum) *Painterly Print*, 33–34.

7. I am deeply indebted to both Tom Woodward, professor emeritus, and Robert Broner, associate professor, Department of Art and Art History, Wayne State University, both printmakers themselves, for help in deciphering some of the techniques used by Bertoia. In addition, the author conducted several experiments with glass plate, oil-based ink, rice paper, brayers, and a variety of instruments to attempt to satisfy herself concerning the possible methods of achieving certain results.

4. Analysis

1. (Metropolitan Museum) *Painterly Print*, ix.

2. Willenbecher, "Harry Bertoia."

3. Harry Bertoia, handwritten notes for a speech given to the Collectors Circle, Virginia Museum of Fine Arts, Richmond, October 14, 1961.

4. Bertoia, conversation with Fairweather and Hoff, tape 4, side B.

5. For a partial list of the artists exhibited, see chap. 1, n. 13.

6. See chap. 1, p. 14.

7. The entire collection became a part of the Bertoia household, at least for a while, after the death of Dr. Valentiner in September 1958, when it was held in trust by Valentiner's daughter for her children. Most of the works were eventually sold or otherwise dispersed.

8. Harry Bertoia to Alida Bertoia, Marie Griffith, and Deli Vetere, n.d. Photostatic copy of handwritten letter signed "Harry" (Bertoia files, Val Bertoia, Barto, Pennsylvania). The letter also reads, in part, "After enjoying the 'Apparition' for many years, at this time in my life, it gives me pleasure to present the painting to you . . . as a gift to be shared and enjoyed alike. Also to remember it to be a token jesture [*sic*] of appreciation to your father and mother."

9. When in 1963 a number of the works from the Valentiner estate were exhibited for sale in Detroit, Bertoia specifically insisted that the Miró was not for sale. The Redons and Klee's *Spiral* were not even exhibited.

10. Quoted in John Rewald, "Odilon Redon."

11. Ibid., 25.

12. George Staempfli to Harry Bertoia, October 23, 1959 (Bertoia files, Val Bertoia, Barto, Pennsylvania).

13. Exchanges were made at other times (e.g., with Josef Albers in 1956), but they were usually initiated by the other artist.

14. The definition is a quotation from André Breton, in (Museum of Modern Art) *Dada, Surrealism*, 63.

15. Bertoia, *Fifty Drawings*.

16. Bertoia, conversation with Fairweather and Hoff, tape 5, side A.

17. Ibid., tape 3, side B.

18. He worked on the sequence for the Bach Toccata and Fugue in D Minor for *Fantasia*. Information concerning the work of Oskar Fischinger (1900–1967) is found in Long Beach Museum, *Bildmusik*, introduction; Moritz, "Oscar Fischinger"; and Los Angeles County Museum, *Spiritual in Art*, 296–311.

19. The friendship of Bertoia and Fischinger was also fueled by their mutual frustration with increasingly idiosyncratic correspondence from Hilla Rebay (Elfriede Fischinger [Oskar's widow], telephone conversation with the author, March 16, 1985, and interview in Los Angeles March 5, 1987).

20. Cass, "Musician's Sculptor."

21. Bertoia, conversation with Fairweather and Hoff, tape 1, side A and tape 5, side B.

22. The Bertoias attended monthly lectures at the Griffith Observatory, and they owned a six-volume set of books on astronomy.

23. Bertoia, conversation with Fairweather and Hoff, tape 1, side A.

24. Lao-Tzu, *Way of Life*, stanza 51.

25. Purchased from Wittenborn & Co., New York City, October 22, 1958.

26. Quoted in Willenbecher, "Harry Bertoia," 7.

27. Of the thirty-four monotypes of the twentieth century shown in the 1980–81 exhibition, "The Painterly Print," including works by artists as diverse as Matisse, Picasso, Dubuffet, Miró, and Jim Dine, only one was as large as thirty by thirty-seven inches—a simple calligraphic dark-field monotype by Robert Motherwell, dated 1976.

28. Johnson, *American Prints*, epilogue.

29. Cass, "Musician's Sculptor."

30. Hans Knoll to Harry Bertoia, October 7, 1953 (Bertoia files, Val Bertoia, Barto, Pennsylvania).

31. Bertoia, *Fifty Drawings*. The statement was written originally in 1976 and was first printed in English in the catalog for Bertoia's exhibition at the Heinie-Onstad Museum in Høvikodden, Norway in that year.

5. The Catalog

THE 1940s

1. Knoll Associates exhibition review.

2. See Nelson, *Harry Bertoia, Sculptor*, pls. 22 and 25.

3. Ibid., pls. 17 and 43.

4. Bertoia, "Drawing."

5. In interviews with the author during 1966 and 1967 (see chap. 2, n. 16), Bertoia more than once mentioned the importance to his work of his associations with various scientists at the Naval Electronics Laboratory at Point Loma.

6. Bertoia, conversation with Fairweather and Hoff, tape 1, side A.

7. It may be of some interest to note that in 1945 the San Francisco Museum of Art (now the San Francisco Museum of Modern Art) ran two special exhibitions simultaneously, one on Bertoia's monotypes and the other on the work of Mark Tobey. Plate 18 has been matted and very well may have been one of those exhibited. Whether or not Bertoia ever made the acquaintance of Tobey is not known. He did meet Jackson Pollock but not until the early 1950s, when he was a frequent guest at the home of Hans and Florence Knoll on Long Island (McGhee, "Influences," 109.)

8. Bertoia, "Light and Structure."

9. The author spent considerable time researching this question in addition to asking the advice of several knowledgeable printmakers, without achieving a definitive answer.

THE 1950s

10. See Nelson, *Harry Bertoia, Sculptor*, pl. 73.

11. Plate 39 is printed on rice paper also, but it is not of the laid variety.

12. The favored oriental paper was Sekishu white, which Bertoia ordered in quantity from the Nelson-Whitehead Paper Company of New York City in the late fifties.

13. See Nelson, *Harry Bertoia, Sculptor*, pl. 76.

14. One horizontal oval is topped by a pyramidal curve in a possible reference to the favorite Bertoia headgear. (See frontispiece.)

15. Descartes attempted to account by a theory of vortices for the formation of the universe and the movement of the bodies composing it.

16. Unfortunately, some of the softness of the composition is lost in the photograph, where the contrasts are much sharper than in the original.

17. Instead of using smooth rods, however, Bertoia created textured ones by welding other materials to their surfaces and brazing them. For examples of these sculptures, see Nelson, *Harry Bertoia, Sculptor*, pls. 27, 31–40, 51, 58, and 83.

18. See ibid., pls. 24 and 25.

19. Bertoia, conversation with Fairweather and Hoff, tape 1, side B.

20. The slide presentation was given at the International Design Conference in Aspen, Colorado in 1955 and at other gatherings subsequently. Its title is one of several uses of the term ''Graphic Poem'' by Bertoia throughout his career.

21. Interview with the author at Bally, Pennsylvania, August 24, 1966.

22. The indentations made by the instrument used for these quick strokes can still be felt on the back of the paper.

23. Bertoia, conversation with Fairweather and Hoff, tape 4, side A. For a further discussion of this sculptural concept, see Nelson, *Harry Bertoia, Sculptor*, 43.

24. Bertoia rarely named his works, sculpture or graphic. However, others sometimes tagged them with names based on their perceived resemblance to natural objects. For examples of these sculptures, see Nelson, *Harry Bertoia, Sculptor*, pls. 27, 52, 63, 64, and 65.

25. See ibid., pl. 73.

26. The print has suffered somewhat from being chewed by mice on its right edge, the result of long storage in Bertoia's barn studio.

27. The thought of using this implement in printing came sometime after 1956, when a new family dog was acquired.

28. See Nelson, *Harry Bertoia, Sculptor*, pls. 28 and 50.

THE 1960s

29. One of the first gongs Bertoia produced was for an American Consulate, in 1956. See ibid., pl. 79.

30. See ibid., pl. 26. The date of 1963, given there, is incorrect.

31. For a description of Bertoia's spill-casting technique, see Campbell, ''Creative Casting.'' For a discussion of the actual casting of the Dulles Airport bronze screen, see Nelson, *Harry Bertoia, Sculptor*, 33–34.

32. See Nelson, *Harry Bertoia, Sculptor*, pl. 39.

33. Ibid., pl. 51.

34. For sculpture fountains done for the Philadelphia Civic Center and the Manufacturers and Traders Trust Company, Buffalo, see ibid., pls. 45–49.

35. A double stem supports the free-standing metal screen done for I. M. Pei's Denver Hilton Hotel in 1961, now in the Denver Museum. It is not nearly as successful as this drawing. See ibid., pl. 56.

36. Ibid., 43–44.

THE 1970s

37. Several unopened packages of this paper remained in Bertoia's barn studio as late as 1983.

38. Since all dimensions of handmade paper are approximate, and torn or cut divisions of a full sheet would, therefore, also vary, I am assuming dimensions of anywhere from twelve to thirteen-plus inches to be one-third of the width and dimensions of up to twenty-five inches to be the height of the original sheet.

39. I am indebted to John Gerard, former Curator of the Cranbrook Academy of Art Museum, for pointing this out.

Bibliography

Books and Catalogs

Allen, Virginia. *Tamarind: Homage to Lithography*. New York: New York Graphic Society, 1969.

Allentown Art Museum, Allentown, Pennsylvania. *Harry Bertoia*. Text by Beverly H. Twitchell. December 14, 1975–February 8, 1976.

Andrew Crispo Gallery, New York. *I. Rice Pereira*. April 17–May 22, 1976.

Baskett, Mary W. *The Art of June Wayne*. New York: Harry N. Abrams, 1969.

Bertoia, Harry. *Fifty Drawings*. Barto, Pennsylvania: Estate of Harry Bertoia, 1980. Privately published.

Bihalji-Merin, Oto [Peter Thoene, pseud.]. *Modern German Art*. Tr. Charles Fullman. Harmondsworth, Middlesex, UK: Penguin, 1938.

Brooklyn Museum, New York. *Thirty Years of American Printmaking*. November 20, 1976–January 30, 1977.

_____. *The American Artist as Printmaker: Twenty-third National Print Exhibition*. Text by Barry Walker. October 28, 1983–January 22, 1984.

Castleman, Riva. *Prints of the Twentieth Century: A History*. New York: Museum of Modern Art, 1976.

Cranbrook Academy of Art, Bloomfield Hills, Michigan. *Cranbrook-"Life" Exhibition of Contemporary American Painting*. Foreword by Archibald MacLeish. May 17–June 2, 1940.

Cranbrook Academy of Art Museum, Bloomfield Hills, Michigan. *The Work of Harry Bertoia*. February 3–24, 1980.

Detroit Institute of Arts, Detroit, Michigan. *Arts and Crafts in Detroit, 1906–1976: The Movement, The Society, The School*. 1976.

_____. *Design in America: The Cranbrook Vision 1925–1950*. December 14, 1983–February 19, 1984.

Elderfield, John. *The Modern Drawing*. New York: Museum of Modern Art, 1983.

Fogg Art Museum, Harvard University, Cambridge, Massachusetts. *Degas Monotypes*. Text by Eugenia Parry Janis. 1968.

Hayter, Stanley William. *About Prints*. New York: Oxford University Press, 1962.

Ivins, William M., Jr. *How Prints Look*. Boston: Beacon Press, 1958.

Johnson, Una E. *Ten Years of American Prints, 1947–1956*. New York: Brooklyn Institute of Arts and Sciences, 1956.

_____. *American Prints and Printmakers*. Garden City, NY: Doubleday, 1980.

Laliberté, Norman, and Mogelon, Alex. *The Art of Monoprint; History and Modern Techniques*. New York: Van Nostrand Reinhold, 1974.

Lao-Tzu. *The Way of Life*. Tr. Raymond B. Blakney. New York: New American Library, 1955.

Long Beach Museum of Art, Long Beach, California. *Bildmusik: Art of Oskar Fischinger*. Text by Richard Whitehall. June 28–July 26, 1970.

Los Angeles County Museum of Art, Los Angeles, California. *The Spiritual in Art: Abstract Painting 1890–1985*. November 20, 1986–March 8, 1987.

Lukach, Joan M. *Hilla Rebay: In Search of the Spirit in Art*. New York: Braziller, 1983.

Metropolitan Museum of Art, New York. *The Painterly Print: Monotypes from the Seventeenth to the Twentieth Century*. Text by Colta Ives, Eugenia Parry Janis, David W. Kiehl, Michael Mazur, Sue Welsh Reed, and Barbara Stern Shapiro. October 16–December 7, 1980.

Museum of Modern Art. *Dada, Surrealism, and Their Heritage*. Text by William S. Rubin. 1968.

Nelson, June Kompass. *Harry Bertoia, Sculptor*. Detroit: Wayne State University Press, 1970.

New Burlington Galleries, London. *First Exhibition of Twentieth Century German Art*. July 8–August 8, 1938.

O'Connor, Francis V. *Jackson Pollock*. New York: Museum of Modern Art, 1967.

O'Connor, Francis V., and Thaw, Eugene Victor, eds. *Jackson Pollock: A Catalogue Raisonné of Paintings, Drawings, and Other Works*. New Haven: Yale University Press, 1978.

Okakura, Kakuzo. *The Book of Tea*. Rutland, VT: C. E. Tuttle, 1956.

Philadelphia Museum of Art. *Paul Gauguin: Monotypes*. Text by Richard S. Field. 1973.

Rasmusen, Henry. *Printmaking with Monotype*. Philadelphia: Chilton, 1960.

Rosenblum, Robert. *Cubism and Twentieth-Century Art*. New York: Harry N. Abrams, 1961.

Sachs, Paul J. *Modern Prints and Drawings*. New York: Alfred A. Knopf, 1954.

St. Paul Art Center, St. Paul, Minnesota. *Drawings USA 1966*. Third Biennial Exhibition, April 7–June 5, 1966.

_____. *Drawings USA*. Fourth Biennial Exhibition, 1968.

St. Paul Gallery and School of Art. *Drawings USA.* First Biennial Exhibition, November 1961.

Seitz, William C. *Abstract Expressionist Painting in America.* Cambridge: Harvard University Press, 1983. Originally presented as Ph.D. diss., Princeton University, 1955.

Soby, James Thrall. *The Prints of Paul Klee.* New York: C. Valentin, 1945.

Sterne, Margaret. *The Passionate Eye: The Life of William R. Valentiner.* Detroit: Wayne State University Press, 1980.

Valentiner, Brigitta. *The Adventure of Living (The Life of Mrs. Harry Bertoia).* Barto, Pennsylvania, 1984. Privately published.

Weitenkampf, Frank. *American Graphic Art.* New York: H. Holt, 1912.

Films and Tapes

Bertoia, Harry. Conversation with Sally Fairweather (gallery owner) and Margo Hoff (artist). September 11, 1978. Tape recording (tapes 1–6, both sides).

Bertoia, Harry. Conversation with Margo Hoff, sound sculptures, n.d. Tape recording (120-minute tape).

Bertoia, Harry (1915–1978). Microfilm, Roll 1471, 166–312, Archives of American Art, Detroit, Michigan.

Eger, Jeffrey. *Sonambients: The Sound Sculpture of Harry Bertoia.* Kenesaw Films, 1971.

West, Clifford B. *Harry Bertoia's Sculpture.* New York: Radim Films, 1965.

Articles and Theses

"Allentown Art Museum, Pennsylvania." Exhibition review. *Art News* 75 (March 1976): 101.

"The American Institute of Architects Awards Harry Bertoia the Craftsmanship Medal." *American Institute of Architects Journal* 25 (May 1956): 213.

Artner, Alan G. "Sounding Out the World of Sculpture's Bertoia." *Chicago Tribune,* February 16, 1975.

Benke, Marjorie. "How to Make a Monotype." *Design,* January 1940, 37.

Bertoia, Harry. "Drawing." *Arts and Architecture* 61 (April 1944): 22–24.

———. "Five Drawings." *Arts and Architecture* 62 (May 1945): 22–23.

———. "Light and Structure." Text of paper presented at International Design Conference, Aspen, Colorado. *Print* 9 (July 1955): 16–17.

"Bertoia at Staempfli." *Arts* 44 (April 1970): 56.

Burrows, Carlyle. "Review of the Non-Objective Painting Show Sponsored by the Solomon R. Guggenheim Foundation." *Christian Science Monitor,* July 24, 1943.

Butera, A. F. "Benjamin Mangel Gallery, Bala-Cynwyd, Pennsylvania, Exhibition." *Arts* 54 (February 1980): 8.

Calabi, Augusto. "The Monotypes of Gio. Benedetto Castiglione." *Print Collector's Quarterly* 10, no. 3 (1923): 221–53.

———. "The Monotypes of Gio. Benedetto Castiglione: A Supplement." *Print Collector's Quarterly* 12, no. 4 (1925): 435–42.

———. "Castiglione's Monotypes: A Second Supplement." *Print Collector's Quarterly* 17, no. 3 (1930): 299–301.

"California Artists." *Art News* 45 (June 1946): 21.

Campbell, Lawrence. "Creative Casting." *Craft Horizons* 23 (November–December 1963): 11ff.

———. "The Monotype." *Art News* 70 (January 1972): 44–47.

Cass, Julia. "A Musician's Sculptor." *Philadelphia Inquirer,* August 10, 1975, Today section.

"The Chemically Pure in Art: W. Hayter, B. Sc., Surrealist." *Art News* (May 15–31, 1941): 13.

Chermayeff, Serge. "Painting toward Architecture." *Arts and Architecture* 65 (June 1948): 31.

"The Circle Is Freed." *Art News Annual* 20 (1950): 146.

Cogle, Henry G. "On Making Monotypes: Part 1." *Artist* 14 (September 1937): 6, 7; "Part 2." 14 (October 1937): 38, 39; "Part 3." 14 (November 1937): 70, 71.

Colby, Joy Hakanson. "Bertoia Works Celebrate the 'Miracle of Life.' " *Detroit News,* February 17, 1980.

"Exhibition at Staempfli Gallery." *Art News* 67 (May 1968): 11.

"Exhibition at Staempfli Gallery." *Arts* 42 (May 1968): 62.

"Exhibition at Staempfli Gallery." *Arts* 44 (April 1970): 56.

"Exhibition at Staempfli Gallery." *Art News* 69 (May 1970): 22.

"Exposition des scultures et graphismes chez Knoll International France." *Aujourd'hui* 8 (April 1964): 96, 97.

Forman, Nessa. "Honoring the Best the Arts Have to Offer—Harry Bertoia: For His Sculpture." *Philadelphia Bulletin,* April 13, 1980.

Frankenstein, Alfred. "Tobey and Bertoia: Fantasy and Geometry." *Art News* 44 (October 1, 1945): 28.

Glueck, Grace. "Harry Bertoia, 63: Sculptor, Designer." Obituary. *New York Times,* November 8, 1978.

Knoll Associates exhibition review. *Art News* 51 (January 1953): 44.

McGhee, Susan Joyce. "Influences Affecting the Nurturing of the Artist-Craftsman—Harry Bertoia." Masters thesis, Pennsylvania State University, 1971.

Moholy-Nagy, László. "The New Bauhaus, American School of Design, Chicago." *Design,* March 1939, 19.

"Monoprints at Nierendorf Gallery." *Art Digest* 21 (April 15, 1947): 22.

"Monotypes: What They Are; How They Are Made." *Art Instruction*, May 1938, 16–17.

Moore, E., ed. "Letters from Thirty-one Artists to the Albright Knox Gallery." *Albright Knox Gallery Notes* 31–32, no. 2 (Spring 1970): 6–7.

Moritz, William. "The Films of Oskar Fischinger." *Film Culture* 58–60 (1974): 37–187.

Naylor, Blanche. "What's Going On." *Design*, November 1939, 32.

Nelson, George. "Notes on the Monotype: A Few Experiments with a Neglected Medium." *Pencil Points* 18 (1937): 785–92.

Nierendorf Gallery exhibition review. *Art News* 43 (February 1, 1945): 25.

Nierendorf Gallery exhibition review. *Art News* 46 (May 1947): 48

Obituary. *Interior Design* 50 (January 1979): 50.

Obituary. *Interiors* 138 (January 1979): 24.

"Review of Loan Exhibition on Third Floor of Museum of Non-Objective Painting." *Art Digest* 18 (November 1, 1943): 12.

Rewald, John. "Odilon Redon." In *Odilon Redon, Gustave Moreau, Rodolphe Bresdin.* New York: Museum of Modern Art, 1961.

Rice, William S. "Monotyping by Another Method." *Art Instruction*, July 1938, 21.

Riley, Maude. "Monoprints by Bertoia." *Art Digest* 19 (February 1, 1945): 19.

Review of Staempfli Gallery exhibition, New York. *Arts* 47 (February 1973): 88.

Review of Staempfli Gallery exhibition, New York. *Art News* 75 (December 1976): 125.

Review of Staempfli Gallery exhibition, New York. *Art News* 78 (January 1979): 141.

Stevens, Dr. William O. "Understanding Modern Art: More Discussion of Those Carnegie International Awards." *Art Instruction*, June 1938, 18.

Wheelock, Warren. "Understanding Modern Art: A Discussion of Jacques Villon's 'The Philosopher.' " *Art Instruction*, May 1938, 27.

Willenbecher, John B. "Harry Bertoia, a Monograph." Honors thesis, Brown University, 1958.

Wolf, Ben. "At Nierendorf Gallery." *Art Digest* 20 (December 15, 1945): 10.

Index

June Kompass Nelson received her B.A. from Drexel University, Philadelphia, her M.A. in art history from Wayne State University, and studied at the Accademia di Belle Arti and the Università degli Studi, Facoltà di Lettere e Filosofia, both in Florence. She has taught at Wayne State University and at the University of Michigan, Dearborn. She has written several articles and is the author of *Harry Bertoia, Sculptor.*

The manuscript was edited by Michael Lane. The book was designed by David Ford. The typeface for the text is Palatino. The display type is Palatino. The book is printed on 70-lb. Sterling Litho Matte and is bound in Holliston's Roxite Vellum over binder's boards.

Manufactured in the United States of America.